THE
INVESTMENT
REVOLUTION

THE
INVESTMENT
REVOLUTION

HOW TO TAKE
CONTROL OF YOUR
FINANCIAL FUTURE

FRANCIS GINGRAS ROY

Forbes | Books

Published by Forbes Books, Charleston, South Carolina.
An imprint of Advantage Media Group.

Forbes Books is a registered trademark, and the Forbes Books colophon is a trademark of Forbes Media, LLC.

Printed in the United States of America.

10 9 8 7 6 5 4 3 2 1

ISBN: 978-1-64225-693-2 (Hardcover)
ISBN: 978-1-64225-692-5 (eBook)

Library of Congress Control Number: 2024910932

Book design by Megan Elger.

This custom publication is intended to provide accurate information and the opinions of the author in regard to the subject matter covered. It is sold with the understanding that the publisher, Forbes Books, is not engaged in rendering legal, financial, or professional services of any kind. If legal advice or other expert assistance is required, the reader is advised to seek the services of a competent professional.

Since 1917, Forbes has remained steadfast in its mission to serve as the defining voice of entrepreneurial capitalism. Forbes Books, launched in 2016 through a partnership with Advantage Media, furthers that aim by helping business and thought leaders bring their stories, passion, and knowledge to the forefront in custom books. Opinions expressed by Forbes Books authors are their own. To be considered for publication, please visit **books.Forbes.com**.

I DEDICATE THIS BOOK TO

My life partner, Audrey Ann, who supports me in my busy life between my business and my passions. She takes care of our family and gives me peace of mind. The old saying is true, "Behind every great man there's a great woman."

My two daughters, Sofia and Olivia, who give me daily motivation to strive for and a future to look forward to.

My current clients who have trusted me from the beginning. You are the reason why I wake up all fired up in the morning.

My future clients: I look forward to working with you to help achieve your goals.

CONTENTS

FOREWORD

Francis has put together a masterpiece that will greatly contribute to the investment community at large and his clients individually. This book will shed light, in tremendous fashion, on his knowledge and wisdom while giving you insights into Francis's life experiences and his generosity in giving back to his community.

When working with a wealth management advisor, "authenticity" and "goodwill" are two words that come to mind. When the advisor demonstrates these characteristics, magical things can happen. Francis *is* a man of authenticity and goodwill, as proven by his personality and diligent work ethic. I have known Francis for more than ten years, and I can attest to his passion and zeal as a wealth management advisor and the extraordinary value he delivers to everyone he is in contact with, personally and professionally.

There is a wealth of must-learn information contained in this book for any investor who is serious about having input on their financial future. Francis addresses questions that *must* arise and provide clear and concise answers that will give you peace of mind. He is thorough in his journey to uncover financial value for his clients, leaving no stone unturned in his research, leading to confidence in his recommendations. His clients have always found security in Francis's ability to provide guidance in an easy-to-follow style, knowing that he has thoroughly studied any information/recommendations he provides.

He follows this same style throughout this book, writing in very clear and plain language, allowing you to uncover unique concepts and advice that are as valuable as rare gems. Francis truly excels in finding "five quarters" in a dollar for his clients.

What's so impressive is that the "little things" can have such a great impact on your financial future, which says that, in the final analysis, there really is no such thing as insignificant details. Keep your eyes and mind wide open because you will benefit from *everything* you read in this book!

Sincerely,

Camille Estephan
Senior Investment Advisor, Branch Owner
Diligence Wealth Management

ACKNOWLEDGMENTS

Camille Estephan, a true leader and business mentor. Your wise advice and continued support have helped me go through the toughest times of life. Your strength of character inspires me every day.

Thierry Jabbour, you gave me the opportunity of a lifetime, you truly changed my life path forever, and I will always be grateful for this.

My mother's ex-husband, **Pierre**, you have been a father to me and you gave me so many opportunities. All the traveling I was able to do when you hired me to work for the Formula One (F1) and the Professional Golf Association (PGA), our trips to China and Europe to shop for patio furniture—these made me who I am today. I thank you for teaching me that things could be different when you "dare to be different" as you always told me.

My parents, who gave me all the love and comfort a child needs while growing up. You always supported my different life experiences, even though you didn't always agree with my choices, but you always respected my decisions and treated me as an equal. You gave me the confidence to achieve whatever I set my mind to.

My fiancé and life partner, **Audrey Ann**, for being so understanding with my busy and ambitious life. I couldn't do it without you!

INTRODUCTION

Dear Reader,

Hello and welcome to the world of wealth management!

As your personal investment advisor, it's my pleasure to help you set goals that move you toward obtaining your financial freedom so that you can live the life that you want today *and* in the future!

To my clients who are forty-five to sixty-five years old, you are living in the sweet spot of life. You're in a great career. You have a loving family. And you have money to save and spend in the present while also contributing to your retirement.

To my clients who are already retired, you are truly living your golden years. With debt in the rearview mirror, you have the opportunity to travel, volunteer, or whatever is in your heart to do—all because you are financially set.

To those who are considering becoming a client, I welcome you to be part of my financial family. You have dreams and goals, and together, with the right planning, we can make these a reality.

For most people, financial freedom seems to be an elusive goal. There are weekly and monthly bills to pay, long-term mortgages and car loans, and so many other demands on their finances that they wonder at times how they are ever going to keep up, let alone get ahead. But financial freedom isn't just about eliminating your financial obligations; weekly and/or monthly expenses such as groceries, gas for your car, and so on are an ongoing part of life. What financial freedom entails is having the finances to pay off long-term debt and save for the future while enjoying life today! As one of my clients, you already understand this philosophy. And if you're considering becoming a client, this type of freedom can be a reality, and I can help you achieve it.

As you go through this book, you'll read about my journey to becoming a financial wealth management advisor so that you can get to know me personally. These chapters are interspersed with chapters containing educational and practical investment knowledge, giving you a solid understanding of different types of investments and philosophies.

My personal journey starts with my story of a kid growing up in middle-class Quebec, who always wanted to be financially independent; I didn't want to rely on working for someone else my entire life but wanted financial freedom provided by my own businesses and investments. Mine isn't a rags-to-riches story or one in which I've had the proverbial Midas Touch. My ability to manage wealth has come through education, discipline, and hard work, the same path you have taken to get where you are today.

Like most of you, I didn't grow up wealthy. And like some of you, I grew up with divorced parents. I didn't lack any of the basic necessities, but there wasn't a lot of money left over.

Early in my adult life, I struggled to figure out the what-seems-to-be elusive goal of financial independence. But I knew it was achievable. I've always been a productive person, even as a kid. I was never one to waste time. I also wanted to move out of the house as soon as possible. Even though my parents were not together, they both loved me and never pressured me. My mom and I lived in a nice house as did my dad. But I wanted to be responsible for myself. I wanted to save. To pay bills. To be an adult and the captain of my own future. Even when I was doing fun things, I had a purpose in mind. So, you might say I've always lived a purpose-driven life.

Ever since the age of ten, I would do whatever I could to earn money, and I always put half of it away. I don't know where I learned that; to me, it was a natural thing to do. While many of my friends were at summer day camps, I was earning money to buy my first gas-powered scooter so that I could drive wherever I wanted and have my first taste of independence.

At sixteen, I had saved and earned enough money—along with selling my scooter—to purchase a 2001 Honda CR 125. Boy, was I the envy of all my friends! I was also making a budget to live on. (What sixteen-year-old in their right mind does that?) I had my income, expenses, and savings down to a tee. For every $2 in income, $1 went to expenses and the other dollar toward savings. This is where I began to learn the value of compound interest, which is the "holy grail" of financial freedom, and something I'll discuss in detail in this book. This save-and-work-to-upgrade mentality has always been part of my makeup. My mom saw this in me and realized I was a responsible person, so she bought me my first car at sixteen, a 2002 Pontiac Sunfire. Thanks, Mom!

I also told my mom that I wanted to be financially independent by age thirty. I didn't have a clue how to achieve this, but I knew it was possible, and this goal burned in my heart. It was like I had a vision that kept calling to me.

I'm not sure why, but I was born with this type of drive, which has been a disadvantage at times and an advantage at other times. For example, when I was in school, I wanted to get a perfect grade on every test. At the private school I attended, we had year-end exams to prepare us for high school. While studying, my need to be the best caused me to put so much pressure on myself that I nearly passed out on the day of the exams! But that same drive always made me endlessly curious about almost everything, giving me a thirst for knowledge. I've never had a know-it-all attitude, and I've always been willing to learn from others, anywhere, anytime. Even today, this mentality serves me well in the financial field; I'm always learning and growing my knowledge of finances and the way they work.

Business and finances have always piqued my interest. From running my own small businesses during summers throughout my high school years to my providential meeting with Camille Estephan—which was the start of my wealth management business—my life has been focused on growing my finances so that I could chart my own course in life. Along the way, I've maintained a mindset of helping others whenever and wherever I can.

You will also educate yourself as you read the chapters on financial aspects that are not typically covered in this type of book. I will help you to understand the different mindsets about investing so that you can understand the way you think and why you think the way you do. I'll give you a solid understanding on specific types of investments such as ESG—environmental, social, and governance—and an overview of cryptocurrencies, both of which are important topics to the younger generations and that older individuals want to know about.

Finally, I would be doing you a disservice if I didn't tell you about investment options that you have and my opinion on these vehicles. Chapter 14, "Investing for Success," will give you this information. At the end of these chapters, you can record your thoughts on what you've learned and how the information applies to your financial situation.

Are you ready? Then pour your favorite beverage, settle into your easy chair, and turn to the next page. You're about to start on a financial journey that can literally change your life!

Your wealth management partner,

Francis Gingras Roy

CHAPTER 1

HOW A BRIEF RETAIL STORE OWNERSHIP CHANGED EVERYTHING

Perspective is a moment in time that cannot be fully appreciated until that moment has passed.

—TIBOR KALMAN

Ever since the age of ten, I've wanted to be financially independent. If you think about it, that's a strange goal for a ten-year-old boy. Most kids that age are playing video games, involved with sports, and hanging out with friends. Sure, I had lots of friends, and we did stuff together like riding bikes, playing road hockey, and stay over at one another's houses. But I was also focused on earning and saving money. I'm not sure why I had this mindset, but I wanted to achieve financial independence by the age of thirty. I was always a good student in school and got good grades, but I had no idea of the exact path to take to make my goal a reality. What I did know was that becoming an entrepreneur, a business owner, was the right direction for me.

As I started down the entrepreneurship road, I thought that real estate would be my golden ticket, so I began doing a lot of research.

I purchased a triplex for $390,000, which I kept for seven years. When I sold it for $425,000, I didn't make much of a profit, but the intervening years taught me a lot about how money and real estate investments work and don't work, and I learned from my mistakes. While I continued to invest in real estate, I realized it was not a financial avenue that I wanted to pursue full time.

A year or so into my real estate foray, I thought that general contracting might be the direction for me to take. My mom and her husband at the time, Pierre, who was like a second dad to me, had several businesses, one of which was general contracting, but she told me this was an expensive field to get into and expensive to maintain a business. What was I to do?

After much thought and consideration, I decided to become an electrician so that I could have my own electrical business. I've always liked working with my hands, so this seemed like a good fit. Once I had my electrician's license and started working for a contractor, I realized that buying material, getting permits, and running the business while doing the actual work quickly turned me off, so I still wasn't happy.

While working full time as an electrician for another company, I had a conversation with my mom's husband, who casually mentioned that he was going to China for a trade show to look into the possibility of importing patio furniture.

I said, "Great. I'm going to China with you."

A couple of weeks later, we were at the Canton Fair making contacts. Soon after, we started importing containers of patio furniture and had opened a store. The next year, we attended a huge business fair in Cologne, Germany, to make contacts and find better quality merchandise. We had a much better idea of what our customers wanted, and we were determined to meet their needs.

In between the China and Germany trade shows, I was working full-time hours during the day as an electrician and spent my evenings in the patio store. I had also taken out a loan for my share of the patio business, so I was now in debt. And I hated debt! After much thought, I decided to sell my pickup truck that I owned free and clear to help pay down my debt, and I bought a cheap car for $1,500 to keep me on the road.

The problem with selling patio furniture is it's a seasonal business. We made good money for six months of the year, but we had inventory and other expenses the rest of the year to cover, so there wasn't much money to be made overall. As a young man, I felt I was spinning my wheels and not going anywhere toward finding a business that was right for me.

One Saturday in the spring of 2014, I was working in the patio store as a salesman. It was a slow afternoon, and I was looking out the storefront windows, when I watched a Jaguar F type pull up. I have always loved cars, so the Jaguar caught my immediate attention. A man then came in, who introduced himself as Thierry. We struck up a conversation about his car, and when I casually asked him what he did for a living, he said, "I work as an investment advisor."

An hour later, he walked out after purchasing some unique patio furniture sets, and he left me asking myself, "What is an investment advisor?"

A month later, I delivered the furniture to Thierry's house. Was I impressed! He lived in a gorgeous house on the lake, and I had never known anyone who had this type of success. I normally didn't make deliveries, but my delivery guy wasn't available that day, so I had to do this myself. I believe that it was meant to be! After setting up the patio furniture in his impressive backyard backing onto the lake, Thierry asked, "Is the patio furniture your company?"

"Yes," I replied, "I have a 25 percent stake, and I also work full time as an electrician until I develop the patio business into a full-time income. I want to grow the business so that I can have outlets across the province."

"Hmm, you have discipline and ambition," Thierry replied. "I'd like to see you in the financial services industry."

I looked at him and tilted my head. "I didn't know you could be an entrepreneur in the financial services industry. I thought it was limited to working in a bank."

Thierry smiled. "There are investment advisors outside of the banking world, like those at the brokerage firm where I work. The place to start is by obtaining your Canadian securities license, then you can work with me. I will show you everything you need to know to become a successful investment advisor." Then he looked at me with serious eyes. "The key is to always add value to others and to focus on what is best for their financial situation. Does that make sense to you?"

I thought about his words for a few minutes and then said, "Sure, I understand. As an electrician, I'm always thinking ahead about the work I'm doing for a homeowner, and making sure it is exactly what the person wants. As a salesman in my patio furniture store, I don't try to oversell or sell someone something they don't really want, so that I can make a buck. Even as a kid when I was making money, I wanted to make sure the people I was working with were happy."

Thierry smiled. "That's great to hear."

I still wasn't clear on the difference between working at a bank and working for a brokerage firm, so Thierry took several hours over a few days to help me understand. I was now intrigued and said, "I'm in!"

"Excellent!" replied Thierry. "Why don't you come down to my office, and we'll have another talk?"

I left his house in a daze. On my way home, I called one of my best friends, who was also named Francis, and told him all about meeting Thierry.

A few days later, I went to see Thierry at his office. We talked for a couple of hours during which he helped me to sign up for the securities course. A week later, I had registered. I was now working up to forty hours a week as an electrician and about twenty hours a week at the patio store while cramming to study for the securities course.

I was literally working and studying day and night! I knew that becoming an entrepreneur in the financial world was the right road for me to take, and I was determined to be successful. My work ethic also compelled me to continue doing solid work as an electrician and to make sure the patio store was running efficiently.

About mid-August, the boss who owned the electrical company met me one morning before I went off to work. "You're not your normally energetic self these days," he said.

He was right. I was dragging myself into work, dog-tired. "I've just got a lot going on right now," I told him.

"OK, but I'm concerned about you, so you need to figure out what's going on in your life."

By the end of the summer, I knew exactly what I wanted to do. I handed in my resignation. I was ready to dive into the wealth management field.

My life had turned a corner, and I was about to take a road that I knew would lead to financial freedom, and I could help others achieve the same. It would take hard work and sacrifice, but I was prepared.

Over the course of the summer, I had several conversations with Thierry to prepare myself mentally and financially. He let me know that I was starting from the ground in a commission-based position and that, even though he would be supporting and educating me, I had to budget my money. "It takes a lot to get people to trust you with their finances," he said, "so be prepared for some lean times as you start out."

At that time, I had a mortgage on my condo that I co-owned with a friend and was only working part time at the patio store. So, I cut back on everything I could to make sure my bills were paid and only used my credit card when necessary. I also studied hard for the next several months before I felt I was ready for the securities exam.

The Canadian Securities Course is conducted by the Canadian Securities Institute for individuals interested in trading securities or providing investment advice. The first two exams consisted of one hundred questions each. They were spread over two days, a couple of hours each day, and were taken in person. The third exam was the CPH—Conduct and Practices Handbook Course. I was so nervous over the three days! My entire future would hinge on passing, but I was also confident and prepared. At the end of the third day, I had my results via computer. I had passed the exams! I could go back to Thierry and tell him I was ready to start.

I also did something that would have been unthinkable before meeting Thierry. I called Pierre and said, "I've enjoyed working with you in the patio furniture business, and I've made sure that it is running smoothly from my end. However, I've decided it's time for me to move on, and you can keep my shares." Just like playing poker, I was going all in, and I was grateful that my family was supportive of my decision.

On a September Monday morning, as Thierry and I shook hands, I had a gleam in my eye that said I was determined to learn and work hard. After a couple of minutes of small talk, Thierry and I walked into a conference room, where I joined a group of eight new-to-the-field individuals. I sat down at my desk, fired up my newly purchased laptop, and took a deep breath. "This is it!" I told myself.

I glanced at the person on my right and nodded a hello. Then I turned to the person on my left and grinned. There was my friend, also named Francis, dressed in a suit with his computer open. I thought back to the string of conversations we had following my talks with Thierry over the summer. Francis felt the timing was right for him to become an investment advisor as well. He had passed his securities exam shortly after me, and we had spent an evening celebrating. Now we were sitting side by side!

To say I was intimidated would be an understatement. That first day, we found out that Thierry was one of the top guys in wealth management in all of Canada. And we soon learned that his reputation preceded him everywhere within the company. For me, I felt an extra burden; I didn't want to let him down.

A week later, we were moved from the conference room to business cubicles. I was determined to be successful and was determined to be the hardest worker in the group. Each of us was given a list of two thousand names with residential phone numbers. We were also given a script and told that we should be making five hundred calls/day. Our hours were nine o'clock in the morning to nine o'clock in the evening.

And that's where my career as an investment advisor started.

I was shy at first, not wanting to say the wrong thing. But after three days, I found a groove and my comfort level increased. Soon, I didn't need a script and making these cold calls became second nature. I was eating my breakfast, lunch, and dinner in my cubicle, making more and more calls. Without knowing it, I was fast becoming one of the best junior advisors within the company. I was meeting new clients with Thierry, learning from him how to genuinely care about our clients and to always have their financial welfare at heart. His attention to detail and his knowledge of the industry were impressive, but he never came across as being superior in any way. Thierry was a man who lived the same values and ideals that I wanted to share with my clients.

Every day it was the same schedule. Come into my cubicle and start calling prospective clients. Not everyone in our group was cut out for this type of work, and several people quit after a few weeks. But when I look back on those days, I realize I was laying a foundation that has stood me well over all these years.

I learned to be comfortable talking to complete strangers about one of the most emotional topics there is: money. I learned to listen, to respect what the other person was saying, and to genuinely care about people. I wasn't talking about a livelihood; I was talking about life because, for most people, money is their life. My *job* was to book meetings and do follow-up calls to make sure the individual(s) showed up. But this was more than just a job to me. I wanted to help people change their lives and lifestyles so that they could live the life they wanted to.

In Canada, the majority of people have their financial investments with their local bank. My struggle with the banking industry is that each of the big banks is a publicly traded company, and as such they are in business to make money for their shareholders. In the big picture, a financial advisor at a bank is there not only to sell products and services that meet the client's needs but also to make a profit for their bank.

I quickly understood the difference between a bank selling a financial investment based on its limited portfolio and being able to help clients choose what is best for them based on an almost unlimited choice of funds, stocks, bonds, life insurance, and more. During my initial calls, I felt good explaining the difference between what an independent broker can offer and how a bank is limited in its portfolio. That meant I did not have any "inventory," so I didn't try to "sell" a prospective client any particular investment. This allowed me to get to know each client individually and personally and to understand their current financial situation and what they were looking for in the future *before* talking about any investments that could help them achieve their financial goals.

Having a client-centered focus came naturally to me, whether on the phone or meeting in person. I could research a multitude of investments and create a custom plan for each individual. Being an investment advisor at a brokerage firm meant that I could maintain objectivity, always doing my best for my client. I wasn't being paid a salary or a sales commission. I would earn my income based on a percentage of the portfolio that I managed for each client. The greater the return, the more my clients would make, and the more I would make.

Our interests were aligned, and that's the most simple and honest way of doing business in the financial world. This gave me confidence to talk to people about their finances, because I truly believed that what I was doing was the right thing, and, over the years, my clients have told me they can "feel" this about me. So, I learned early in my career to always do what is best for my client; doing so would turn out the best for me. That's financial karma, and to this day it's my "secret sauce."

In the early weeks of my career, whenever I contacted someone who was interested in talking about their finances and investing, I would build a profile on who they were, their vocation and salary, and their family situation (and I still do this today). I would then book a meeting in which Thierry would either have a retirement plan mapped out for them, based on the profile I gave him, or he would review their current retirement plan to see where they could save or make them more money, based on their financial objectives. For example, if someone had an existing retirement plan and advisor but was looking for a second opinion, we might be able to save money on service-related fees they were paying or could show them better-performing funds and individual stocks that were more in line with financial goals and their risk tolerance.

I always took good mental notes on how Thierry interacted with the individual(s); I wanted to learn from the best so that I could be the best! I never saw him exaggerate what we had to offer, and I made myself a promise to follow his example.

One of the great things about being an investment advisor is offering clients an array of financial help, including tax lawyers, estate lawyers, and accountants, as well as products such as life insurance. All of these are a great benefit to clients, and Thierry knew this well. After a few weeks, he started taking me with him to meet prospective clients, and, without resorting to salesmanship, he would explain various offerings and leave the decision up to the individual. This was another great lesson when working with people that I learned from him. Ideally, he would become the client's go-to person for anything related to finances.

Working with Thierry became my life—fourteen hours a day for the next few months. But, as I've said, I wanted to learn from the best to be the best.

Typically, it takes a junior advisor three to four years to become independent so that they can start building their own clientele. However, after seven months, I felt I was ready mentally and emotionally, and I had the knowledge to meet with prospective clients on my own.

One morning, I came into Thierry's office and sat across from him.

"I'm ready," I said.

"Ready for what?" he asked.

"I'm ready to go out on my own, to have my own desk, just like you."

He sat back and stared at me for a few moments. Then he smiled. "I've known you're ready for a couple of weeks, but you had to come to that realization yourself."

We spent the next couple of days going over the requirements of being independent. I went home that night knowing I was on the right track; the visionary mindset I had at age ten was starting to come into view. However, I was extremely nervous. Thierry would not be there to guide me when talking to a client, so all the responsibility fell on my shoulders. I didn't have the practical experience that he did, and I felt like a lawyer who was getting ready to present my first case in a public courtroom. The spotlight was now on me.

There was lots of paperwork to review and software to learn, and I had yet to develop my own style of working with clients. To be truthful, my first couple of meetings with clients were not the best; I talked too quickly and forgot several important points. Over the next couple of days, I reviewed all that I learned from Thierry: the way in which he initially met and talked with a client; how he followed up in the second meeting with a presentation; the retirement plan he would then show in the third meeting. He used the same approach over and over so that he could determine how to tailor the client's wealth management to their needs. I reminded myself that I had been in so many of these meetings with him that I could almost say word for word the same things he would say.

Remembering the format to follow settled my nerves, and my next meeting with a new client went well. After that, my confidence grew, which further calmed me down. I started to really listen to my clients, to hear their needs, their desires, their goals. I could then create an individual financial plan that worked for them.

As the weeks and months went by, I became more and more comfortable and confident in myself and my skills. I had learned from the best, Thierry, but I was also ready to put my own stamp on my position as an investment advisor. For instance, the office policy was "no beards allowed" and "ties were mandatory." But I had a beard and wasn't one for wearing ties.

Thierry was willing to give me some space and see if these types of changes affected my success rate. I don't know if they helped, but they certainly didn't hurt because ambition, hard work, and commitment were the keys to my results. If I had questions about a complicated file, he was there to support me, but he mainly left me alone. Within six months, I had become the most successful of the original eight who had joined the company, and I was looked upon as the example for every new investment advisor to follow.

It seemed like everyone we met already had an advisor. Nobody likes to change; nobody likes to get out of their comfort zone. So, it's very tough to convince someone of the benefits of changing, especially when it comes to finances. Whether it's budgeting, saving, spending, or investing, we are creatures of habit.

In this business, rejection is about 98 percent. That's just a cold fact, one that a financial advisor can't take personally, if they want to work in this field in the long run. I reinforce this point over and over with new investment advisors who join my team. Not everyone has the fortitude to keep moving forward, but as the old saying goes, "When the going gets tough, the tough get going."

New advisors must learn to tough it out during the start-up and lean times. I also caution them to realize that people might *say* they will show up for a meeting but may not do so. They might receive a text or email saying, "I changed my mind, or, I spoke to my spouse, and we're not interested." Or the advisor may simply never hear from them again. That happens, so I always prepare my new team members for this eventuality. Taking rejection personally in any form is a recipe for defeat.

I also tell my team that this business is a "numbers game." What I mean is that a financial advisor must make x number of calls to speak to y number of people, which will produce z number of meetings. To this day, I continue to work hard to earn the trust of each and every one of my clients, which is why I value our relationships so much. Trust is always earned, and I remind myself of this every day.

From day one of being an investment advisor, nothing was given to me. In today's world, everyone is on social media talking about the bright side of their lives. But nobody wants to talk about what it takes to get there—to have financial freedom so you can truly live life on your own terms. We see pictures of vacations, but no one says how hard they worked to earn the money to pay for their vacation. Or of the debt they will carry when the vacation ends, if they borrowed the money. I've never lived life that way. My belief is that if I cannot manage my own money, I have no business helping others manage theirs.

Many of my clients have steady incomes as employees. Many others are part-time or full-time business owners. Both have their advantages, but no matter how they earn their income, the path to financial freedom is always the same: proper financial planning for the present and the future, diversification, understanding the value of compound interest, and having a solid and viable retirement plan. Those are the building blocks that I help my clients understand.

TAKEAWAYS

- If you're unsettled in your current job position, let your passion take you to where you want to go, even if you are unclear of where that is.
- Opportunity knocks, but it doesn't always keep knocking; be ready to answer at all times.

- The learning curve at the beginning of anything you want to do is tough, but as the saying goes, "When the going gets tough, the tough get going."

- Not everyone follows through on what they say they are going to do. Don't be that type of person, but be a person of your word.

CHAPTER 2

$3 CAR WASH WEALTH

Success is born out of faith, an undying
passion, and a relentless drive.
—STEPHEN CURRY

By now, you might be wondering, "How does a young man become so financially conscious?" To be honest, I'm not sure where I got this mindset from. I didn't intentionally pursue financial intelligence. I didn't set out to master the power of compound interest. I just know that from the age of ten, when other kids were out riding their bikes, or playing tag, I was focused on making money with the goal of living a life of financial independence. Even though my parents were divorced, I never knew what it was like to lack good food, warm clothing, or a comfortable home. However, I didn't want them taking care of me; I wanted to take care of them!

I can also tell you that I wasn't driven by a sense of insecurity or that I would one day wake up and realize I was destitute. That's important to know, because there are millionaires and even billionaires who feel they are going to run out of money and need to make "just one more dollar." When it comes to finances, insecurity can be an insatiable beast, the cruellest of taskmasters. In my case, I've come to the conclusion that I have always had a visionary mind through which I've understood the almost unlimited benefits that financial freedom can give a person.

The kids my age never understood why I was working while they were away at summer camp. I would just tell them, "I prefer to be more productive and buy what I want to buy. My parents aren't going to give me everything, so I need to make my own money." I had a lot of materialistic goals; for instance, I wanted to buy my first high-end sports car, a Ferrari or a Lamborghini, before age thirty. I was driven. I was ambitious. It was an important dream, an important goal. So, I worked much of the time while other kids were playing. I gained my work ethic naturally; no one forced me, and I still have the same work ethic today. I'm willing to do what other people won't do in order to have what I want to have.

I'm not saying my way was right. Looking back, I realize that I sacrificed some of my childhood; I could have had a lot more fun instead of working so much. So, I can't judge anyone from my childhood who wasn't as ambitious as me. But I know the driving force was much bigger and stronger within me, and I couldn't resist it.

While it might seem like it, money wasn't my driving force either. For instance, if I had a choice between having fun with a bunch of kids and learning from adults, I would have chosen the latter. In many ways, I had an adult mindset while living in a kid's body. At times, I felt guilty because I had such a different mindset than other kids. Yes, I did have some fun, but working and taking responsibility for myself were much more fulfilling.

Of all the kids I grew up with, only one had the same mindset and ambition as me. J-F, short for Jean-François, and I have been the best of friends since we were five years old, and we still are today. He owns a very successful company, and he was the only one like me who was willing to work crazy hours and multiple jobs. As adults, he and I live similar, successful lifestyles, while the kids we grew up with, who were playing street hockey all summer long, are living similar lives to one another. When I think about it, it comes down to the choices we made yesterday that created the lifestyles we all live today.

Another lesson I began to learn by working crazy hours as a kid was the meaning of the word "scaling." I remember thinking that I was working all these hours, but the moment I stopped working, the money stopped coming in. There had to be a better way, but what was it? I didn't want to work more to earn more because that meant all of my waking hours would be doing some type of labour. I've since learned that, with the proper investments working hard for me, I could earn income, whether I was in the office, sleeping at home, or on vacation with my family. This is called "scaling." Scaling occurs when revenue increases without a substantial increase in resources, that is, in my case, the resource being the actual labour I was doing for my job. In other words, I wanted to work smarter, not harder.

If you think about it, as an employee of a company, your income is limited to what you make by your salary. In order to increase your finances, you may need to take on a part-time job or a side business. As an entrepreneur, you might think your ability to earn income is unlimited, but unless you learn how to scale your business, your income is limited by what you can do on your own merits. In both cases, you want your money to work harder so that you can work smarter. Having the right financial platform and the right mix of investments will make your money work hard for you.

As I look back, I do see another driving force in my life. Throughout my childhood and teen years, I was somewhat shy. And I never wanted to be dependent upon anyone. This might sound a little strange, but I never liked the attention of receiving gifts, even for birthdays or at Christmas. To me, receiving a gift felt like I was dependent on someone else. But I can tell you that I *loved* to give! Whether it was a card I created, or a present I was able to purchase with my own money, giving to others filled me with joy.

As an investment advisor today, I can implement my visionary mindset to help others plan for and achieve their own financial independence. In this way, I'm "giving" to them—I'm giving them a path that can lead them to accomplish their financial goals for the present and for the future. Doing so fills me with a deep sense of fulfillment.

I have no doubt that almost any child or young person can learn the basics of financial independence. For every dollar someone gives you, or that you earn, save fifty cents, spend a portion of the remaining money, *and* give a portion of it away. Saving money means you don't have to go into debt unless it's for a major purchase like a house. Spending a portion means you don't have to live like a miserly person. Giving a portion away helps you to be generous toward those less fortunate. I began implementing this financial strategy when I was about twelve years old.

My mother's husband owned a rent-a-car company, and I had the job of washing cars. I would work at his company after school and on weekends, and over the summer I would work forty hours/week.

I earned the princely sum of three dollars per hour, which I was very happy with because I wasn't even old enough to get a job elsewhere, and I was also having fun doing it. During the summer, my mom and my stepdad would encourage me to play with my friends and have fun. But I knew that the key to having fun was having money. With money in hand, I could buy a scooter, a dirt bike, or whatever else I wanted.

As a kid with no driver's license, I had to leave early every morning with my stepdad and come back home pretty late; as the owner of his company, he had to put in long hours. Also, the rental car business was seasonal. I mostly worked at the Dorval Airport location so that we had many Europeans and Americans coming to Canada for their summer vacations.

A couple of years later, I was old enough to switch from cleaning cars to working with my parents on construction sites. They were general contractors and had built a few houses, but they were mainly renovating their own apartment buildings. That's where I've learned that I was pretty good at manual work such as painting, doing new wooden floors, demolishing, and more. I have also switched because there was more money to be made in renovation than in car washing.

Keep in mind that I was a twelve-year-old kid at the time, working forty to fifty hours a week throughout my summer break to earn enough money to invest, to earn interest, and then buy whatever I wanted. At that time, all I wanted was a motorbike. I bought my first scooter at age thirteen, but I was short by $700 to buy the right model that I wanted. So, my mother gave me a loan at 0 percent interest rate (that's a pretty good deal!), and I reimbursed her over the next couple of months by working long hours at the construction sites.

However, the scooter wasn't fast enough for me, so I sold it a couple of months later to buy my first dirt bike. Another couple of months later, I had saved more money, and I was able to sell the dirt bike at a small profit to buy a newer model. I did this many times in a row with the goal of upgrading what I had; I was proud of myself, and I wanted nice things.

Looking back, I think that my motivation for becoming financially independent came from wanting to be able to buy or do whatever I wanted, when I wanted. I wanted to have control over my life and have more options. I remember one year I was at a motocross summer camp for a week with my friends, and there was a guy our age in our group who was a pretty good rider. At the end of the camp, his dad showed up in his pickup truck with a brand-new KTM dirt bike. This was my dream bike, and this kid was getting it as a present! I never found out if it was for his birthday or because he had good grades at school, but I did know that he now had a much better bike than mine. It didn't seem like he had worked hard for it, at least from my perspective.

My parents would have not given me such a gift, and I now thank them because I learned the value of hard work and money. It also gave me a much better appreciation for the things I owned. I needed to take care of my possessions, because repairs were costly. I remember paying a $700 bill, which was a huge amount for a fifteen-year-old to pay, at the garage for repairing my ATV. It was a huge amount for me, but I had no choice to pay it or else the ATV would stay at the garage, and I would not have been able to do what I was basically living for.

It was during my early teens that the power of compound interest entered my life. Whatever I saved each week went into my bank account. While the accumulated interest didn't amount to a lot of extra money, I realized that compound interest was a key to reaching financial independence; it was like someone giving me free money.

I learned about compound interest through the "power of a penny." I'm not sure where I read this as a kid, but here is something that still rings true today.

If you saved a single penny and doubled it every day, then by day thirty, you would have an astounding $5,368,709.12! However, the key is the power of doubling, which is akin to compound interest. If you were to do the same thing but changed the doubling time to just twenty-seven days, you would only have $671,088.64. That's still a lot of money, but it's only 12.5 percent of the thirty-day total.

The mindset of saving every day led me to invest in my first Guaranteed Investment Certificates (GICs) at my local bank. I was under eighteen, so my mother had to be with me, and it was pretty unusual for a guy my age to have any type of investment. After I turned eighteen, I started a professional relationship with my banker, Mike, who was ten to fifteen years older than me. I really liked him, and he was an inspiration to me. He believed in me and would often tell me that I would be very successful because of the habits and interest that I had at such a young age. It was like having my own personal banker, and it felt great to be treated like a successful grown-up! It felt even better because I had built this relationship by myself; I wasn't there because of my parents.

I also think that having entrepreneurial parents was a great advantage to me. As early as eight years old, my father would bring me to work on weekends. I loved spending time with him and watching him work. Back then, my dad had a pager business.[1] To keep me busy, he showed me how to take a pager apart and properly clean it. I appreciated the time he spent with me to teach me valuable business lessons. For instance, I realized that if he was working on a weekend, then someone was depending on him.

At that time, businesses and individuals depended on pagers like we depend upon our cell phones today. Many of those who had pagers were doctors, firefighters, policemen, and other frontline workers, not to mention the countless businesspeople whose businesses needed their attention 24/7. Helping my dad made me realize how dependent people are on one another. And I certainly wasn't going to be the one who let someone else down. So, working for my dad taught me the value of independence *and* interdependence.

My dad, my mom, and her husband were all serial entrepreneurs. Because money was not their focus, they never made it to multimillionaire status; they taught me the value of hard work, self-discipline, having a strong work ethic, and not depending on others. As I look back, having age-appropriate jobs was really internships for me. It was crystal clear that I wanted to be my own boss and depend on myself to get what I wanted and when I wanted it. I wasn't going to be a nine-to-five person; that simply wasn't the way I was built. Together, my parents taught me another valuable lesson: Nobody is going to hand you anything. If you want it, you will work hard to earn it.

As an investment advisor, many of my clients are employed by various companies. The rest are like me and became entrepreneurs. To all of

---

1   A pager, also known as a beeper, when I was a kid, is a handheld wireless telecommunication device that receives and displays alphanumeric or voice messages. Pagers were the forerunners of cell phones.

my clients I say, "Congratulations on choosing the right path for you!" No matter what work-related path a person chooses, their career can lead to financial independence, with the right person at their side. One of the keys is to take a good look at your financial position and determine what you are willing to sacrifice today in order to get where you want to be tomorrow.

There is something else I want to say to all my clients.

When I look back on my life, I think I should have taken the time to have more fun. In some ways, I think I was *too* driven. Financial independence is fantastic to achieve. But don't sacrifice everything just to achieve this goal. I'm glad to tell you that I have learned this lesson. With a young family to take care of, I don't work late into the evenings or on weekends. I enjoy my time with my family, and I also take time for myself, doing things that I enjoy.

Yes, financial independence is important. However, even as young as I am, I realize just how fast life passes. I encourage you to think about how fast your life is going. Then figure out what you enjoy, and with whom, and do what you need to do to fulfill that enjoyment. Certainly, financial freedom is a goal you want to achieve. Just don't wake up one day and realize how much you've missed to accomplish that goal.

I'll close this chapter with a challenge to you. Think about where you are in life right now. Then think about how fast your life is going. Next, ask yourself what you enjoy most in life. Finally, ask yourself how you can achieve the financial freedom you need, in order to do the things you want to do. You just don't want to wake up one day, only to realize how much you've missed in life and then try to figure out how you'll have enough money to get you through the rest of your life.

TAKEAWAYS

- Who you are inside is the true measure of success. Always work on being a person of good character and good conduct.

- Don't judge others; you don't know their motivation. However, judge yourself by asking, "Am I doing the right thing for the right reasons?"

- There are times when you have to sacrifice today for what you want tomorrow.

- Having a "future mindset" is great, but don't live in the future so much that you forget to enjoy life in the present.

CHAPTER 3

CONSTRUCTING A DREAM

If you don't build your own dream,
someone else will hire you to build theirs.
—TONY GASKINS

By the time I was in my early twenties, I was a full-time electrician, had part ownership in a patio furniture business, and was saving money to go into the real estate market. I used my salary as an electrician to pay my bills, to help grow the patio business, and to save money for my real estate investments. This is where I started "scaling" my finances. Most weeks, I was up at five o'clock in the morning, out the door by six, and working through until three o'clock in the afternoon. I'd then go straight to the patio store and work until nine or ten o'clock in the night. Then I would head home, get some sleep, and start this routine over again the next day. I was young. I had the energy. I had the drive. But I knew something was missing—there had to be a better way to make a living and to achieve financial independence.

My business partner was my mom's husband, and I was excited to be in business with him. Given that he was much older than me,

I admired all that he has accomplished in his life. I also wanted to be treated as an adult, so I always gave my fair share of hard work.

As the weeks and months went by, I was getting more and more dissatisfied with my job as an electrician. I also saw myself more and more as a businessman. The patio store was becoming a greater interest to me. I was able to travel to other countries, specifically China, to speak to other business owners and order patio furniture. For instance, I went to the Canton Fair in Guang Zhu, which is the capital of a province in China. The Canton Fair was a huge trade show known all over the world, where everything made in China was on display. One week there might be cars, another week electronics, and another week there was patio furniture. It was there that I made some great business contacts who could design and build the furniture we needed. It was the same concept when I was in Cologne, Germany. This was a very exciting time in my life, and there was certainly a letdown when I returned home to be an electrician again.

For the next couple of years, I attended trade shows in the spring. But I was seeing problems pop up all over the place. One summer, it seemed that we had more rainy days than summer days, and

At the patio furniture warehouse, preparing for some publicity.

our sales were way down, so we were stuck with a surplus inventory that we needed to warehouse. Another problem we faced was international shipping. The containers used to ship the patio furniture were not robust. For instance, we received a container of high-end outdoor umbrellas. However, some of the umbrellas were broken, and others broke after customers purchased them. Of course, there was a demand for a refund, which we had to honour. But getting reimbursed from Chinese companies was a logistical nightmare. Returns entailed shipping the *entire* container of products, along with paying for shipping, which could easily be $5,000–$10,000. Another major problem we faced was the currency exchange rates. While our retail products were sold in Canadian dollars, we had to pay our Chinese suppliers in US dollars. So, we were getting squeezed every turn we took. As well, most of the company representatives spoke little or broken English, so trying to converse with these people was a lesson in frustration.

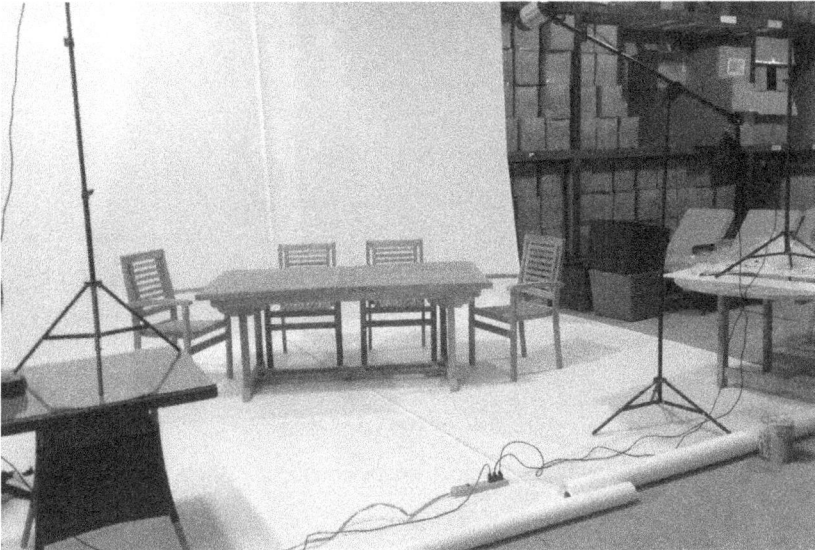

Preparing for publicity pictures at the furniture warehouse.

That first year of business opened our eyes to the reality of our consumer market. I remember our opening day like it was yesterday. We had spent thousands of dollars on advertising, from purchasing a hundred thousand promotion flyers and branded flags for the outside of the store. We had also priced our patio furniture like the well-known, high-end stores that we had studied.

Preparing to take pictures for promotional flyers and door hangers. Thierry received a door hanger at his home and decided to shop at our store for patio furniture.

On opening day, we were full of nervous excitement. But by the end of the day, we were filled with disappointment. With few customers coming through the door and minimal sales, we realized that no one thought of us as a high-end store. And by the end of our first week in business, the stark reality that we were a start-up that no one knew sank into our minds.

Not to be deterred, I delved into market research and came to understand how the public looked at our company—we were a "no-name." Since we didn't have name-brand recognition or an established reputation, we decided to undercut our competition. We created new flyers advertising the company as the "low-end price, high-end quality" patio furniture company. We also spent a lot of money on SEO[2] and digital marketing, such as Google ads, Google keywords, and Facebook ads. This was an expensive way to market, but we knew we had to have a greater online presence to attract customers.

Together, our online marketing began to produce dividends. While foot traffic to the store was slowly increasing, internet sales were taking off. We would routinely sell $2,000 patio sets, meaning inventory stayed low. But this created another problem. We were selling furniture throughout Quebec and into the surrounding provinces, which created delivery problems. We had to rely on local companies that only had an arm's-length agreement with us. Therefore, if there was a problem with the furniture, we had to arrange local and international returns. If we were selling diamond rings, we would have had a good margin to cover all of our expenses. But patio furniture is big and heavy, and the profit margins are small.

The first couple of years in business demanded a lot of work but produced little profit. However, there was another overriding problem. Despite my desire to be a businessman, I quickly realized

---

2   SEO, or search engine optimization, is the process of getting traffic from free, organic, editorial, or natural search results in search engines such as Google. SEO aims to improve a website's position in search result pages. The basic premise is that the higher the website is listed, the more people will see it and will click on the website link.

that patio furniture was not going to be my golden ticket. And to be honest, I had no passion for the business.

In the three years in which I was the co-owner of the patio furniture business, I kept my job as an electrician in order to pay my bills and living expenses. But I was also looking for another business to develop.

One evening, a couple of good friends and I got together for some pizza and business brainstorming. With the experience I had gained dealing with Chinese suppliers, the three of us came up with what we thought was a brilliant idea: iPhone cases that were also bottle openers.

What a brilliant idea—three buddies in business together, selling something we were certain would be a high-demand product. Over the next few weeks, we designed the phone case and came up with colours and branding.

We also had a potential huge local market for our iPhone case/bottle opener: the F1 Grand Prix would be held in Montreal in June. We knew that the F1 circuit had a couple of stops throughout North America, and these were always sold-out events. With Montreal being an international destination, there were sure to be thousands of Canadians, Americans, and Europeans. So, we decided to add the race car team logos to our phone cases. We also planned on hiring several sales reps who would go throughout the venue and across Montreal.

The three of us invested almost all of the money we had. But we were confident in our product and the sales we would have. A week before the Grand Prix was to take place, we had thousands of iPhone/bottle openers in our possession and thirty-five people working for us.

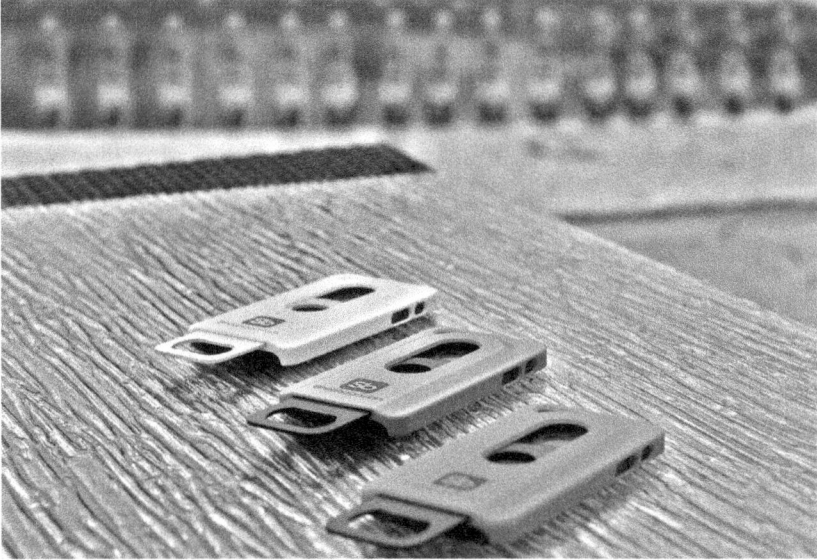

Three different models offered for iPhone case bottle opener.

On Saturday of the Grand Prix weekend, I awoke with high expectations, which were quickly drowned out. I opened the curtain of my bedroom window to see a deluge of rain. As well, the temperature was around a chilly 10°C all weekend. Worst of all, the attendance was one of the poorest on record. Montreal was like a ghost city, and the Grand Prix stadium had a few scattered people in its seats. All the sales reps were very disappointed and also went back home with empty pockets.

Sunday night, my friends and I went home to lick our financial wounds. Over the next few weeks, we sold some of the iPhone cases online, but our dreams of becoming wealthy businessmen went into the garbage, along with most of the phone cases.

Even though I was struggling to find my footing in life and the path that would take me to the financial freedom that I sought, I never gave up. Certainly, there were times of frustration and times I felt almost in complete despair, but I was the type of person who could look defeat straight in the eye, take a deep breath, then ask, "OK, what's next for me?"

I attribute this never-say-die attitude to my ability to always visualize the type of future I was seeking. Visualization—the practice of imagining what you want to achieve in the future—is built into my psyche. I can't give you a reason why, but I've been this way for as long as I can remember. I knew there was a path to success, a path to financial freedom, a path to fulfilling my dreams and goals. I just had to find it.

As an electrician, I was looking to see if having my own electrical contracting business would work for me. As a patio furniture business owner, I thought of franchising even before we opened our first store. And with the iPhone cover/bottle opener venture, I was searching out other potential venues beyond the Montreal Grand Prix, before we had received our first shipment of product.

On top of all of my work obligations, I also worked for Pierre (my mom's ex-husband), who ran a business hiring out limousines and chauffeurs. Looking back, I can see that he was also someone who could visualize what he wanted. He catered to professional sporting events around the world, with the F1 being his major clientele. He also serviced many of the PGA professionals who wanted their own limousine and chauffeur.

During the Montreal Grand Prix, I had the privilege of being one of Pierre's drivers, as well as managing other drivers. Over the next several years, he trusted me enough to fly me around the world to other F1 events, including Spain, Abu Dhabi, and Indianapolis in the United States. An even greater privilege was meeting some of the people involved with F1 racing—from car owners and drivers to people who fly around the world to watch the races. Car racing has always been a passion of mine, which was further fueled with my involvement with the F1 circuit. Being the manager of other drivers, I naturally hired my best buddies; I've always had the mindset of "sharing the wealth."

Being involved with people connected to F1 racing was a surreal experience. They truly live in a different world of wealth and opulence. But I can also tell you firsthand that most of these people were kind and gracious. They knew they had money, but it never "went to their head" so to speak. So, I added this never-look-down-on-anyone mindset to my visualization of what I wanted my life to look like. While searching for my path to financial freedom, I would also help out others whenever I could. And when I found my path to financial freedom, I would make sure that I was helping others reach their freedom as well.

During this time, I dated a girl for a couple of years, who was living in Dubai as a marketing director in the fashion industry. During a trip to the Middle East, I remember telling her all about my experiences and that I wanted to be like these people one day.

She replied, "Oh, honey, you're just an electrician." (As if electricians can't become wealthy.)

But deep down I knew I would be successful, and I used her words as fuel to motivate me. I wasn't in the right place in life, or the line of work that I wanted to be in, but I also knew that if I was patient and continued to visualize what I wanted my life to be like, it would become a reality.

In visualizing my life, it was almost like playing a movie in my mind. I once heard a saying, "Be there before you get there." And that's

Francis and friends, Francis Drolet and Jean-François Charpentier, working for the Abu Dhabi F1 Grand Prix, 2013.

exactly what happens in visualization. There were times when I was at work, driving my car, or at home, and my mind would go off into a world of its own. I would "see" scenes of my life that were exactly what I wanted it to be. I could see the details; I could feel myself in a different context and lifestyle. At times, these types of visualization were almost more real than reality. And when I snapped back to reality, those scenes would stay with me and became embedded in my mind.

I've read that a person's mind cannot distinguish between imagination and reality. That is the reason why, when watching a horror movie, you get scared. You feel threatened, even though there is clearly no danger around you in your cozy living room, as you eat popcorn. But your brain doesn't make the difference. Your mind literally puts you into the movie, and you experience it with all of your senses. The same thing would happen to me during these moments of visualization for my life. I had also read that, unless you can visualize where you want your life to go, and what you want your life to be, you will always remain at the level you are at.

If you think about it, visualization is the key behind every invention that has become a reality throughout the ages. A "problem" is the reality, but somebody somewhere envisions a "What if?" That person then follows their "What if?" down a path that is full of ups and downs. But their never-say-never attitude and their envisioned solution eventually lead them to a solution to the original problem and thus the invention they had visualized. This type of thinking also brings up another saying I've heard: everything starts in the mind.

Throughout my twenties, visualization was the fuel that drove my life and drove me to seek what I knew was possible: financial freedom and independence. I just had to find the path that would lead me to my "promised land."

When I eventually met Thierry, little did I know that he would hand me the key that would turn my visualization into reality. You can say that our meeting was by chance, but, looking back, I can tell you that destiny led to our first meeting, in response to what I visualized my life to be.

Thierry had received one of the hundreds of thousands of flyers advertising the grand opening to my patio furniture business. Intrigued by our products, he came into the store, and we struck up a conversation that eventually led to talking about the Jaguar he drove and his lifestyle. At the end of our conversation, he invited me to take a look at his financial business so that I could consider whether or not this was the right path for me. Meetings like this are simply too good to be true. And I'm convinced that meeting Thierry was a result of my constant visualization of what I wanted my life to be like. I was open to new possibilities. As the saying goes, "Be ready when opportunity comes knocking."

And I was ready.

TAKEAWAYS

- The saying, "The early bird gets the worm," is true in any facet of business.
- Knowledge will tell you who you want to be; hard work will get you where you want to go.
- Your passion and purpose are always intertwined.
- Visualize what you want your life to be every day and what you want your life to be into the future.
- Whatever the mind believes to be true, it also believes this will become a reality.

CHAPTER 4

FIVE HUNDRED CALLS A DAY

Success is focusing the full power of all you are on what you have the burning desire to achieve.

—**WILFRED PETERSON**

A couple of weeks after completing my orientation under Thierry's direction, I came in early and sat at my desk. With a coffee in my hand, I sat back to think about all that had happened in such a short time. Then I smiled; my life had turned a corner. While I enjoyed the physical labour that comes with being an electrician and running a patio furniture store, I was now doing a different type of work. I was using my people skills and engaging my mental capacity. Even more important was the fact that I now believed in what I was doing. I also believed that I had found the life path I had been seeking for the last several years.

I have always loved finances and understanding how they worked and how money—when handled properly as a tool to improve life—can truly be a blessing. In my previous lines of work, I had to do everything myself. But I was surrounded by a team of experts, and I was like a sponge whenever I was in my mentor's presence. I asked questions, lots of them, but I mainly listened with the mindset to learn.

An advantage I feel I had over my team members was the fact that this wasn't my first job. In contrast, this was the first full-time job for my team members. Often, I would hear one of them say, "This is hard work!" And I would nod and smile, thinking, "We get to sit at our desks, make phone calls, and talk to people. You don't know what hard work is."

My previous jobs had taught me the value of having a strong work ethic. I had always worked hard, day in and day out, sometimes double shifts as an electrician, and always spending time in the evenings and weekends at the patio furniture store. At times, I was in minus 30° C weather; other times it was plus 40° C, but I never stopped. I applied that same work ethic to my job as a wealth management advisor.

So, what did my team members consider hard work? Each and every weekday, we were tasked with twelve-hour shifts and making five hundred cold calls a day. We each had a desk in a climate-controlled office, with a lunchroom and fresh coffee when we wanted. Compared with the years I spent eating my lunch in my truck and drinking coffee from a thermos, I almost felt like I was in "work heaven."

Five hundred calls a day, from nine o'clock in the morning to nine o'clock in the evening. I was ready for this type of hard work.

One Monday morning, about eight o'clock, I was getting ready to start my day. One of the senior advisors approached me and said, "Francis, you are the first one here and the last to leave every single day. And you hit your five hundred calls/day quota every day. Don't you find this work hard? What drives you to do this?"

I then told him about my life and work history and wrapped it up by saying, "Now I get to work at a job that I enjoy and have my weekends off. What more could I ask for?"

The advisor smiled and said, "You're going to go far in this business."

The hardest part about this business—and what my team members complained the most about—was the constant rejection.

But there were two specifics that kept me going, besides my work ethic. The first was that I always kept my end goal in mind—financial freedom for the clients I worked for and myself. The second was the continual mentoring from Thierry. In my mind, he was the poster boy for success. I rarely saw him down or in a bad mood. He also taught me that, "Rejection is simply part of this business and part of life. The quicker you accept that, the better you will do." So, I took on this mindset. If I was rejected after the first call, the hundredth call, or the four-hundredth call, I simply dialed the next number on my list.

During the first week of our orientation, we were all asked if we had a business plan or knew what one was. No one raised their hand. One of the senior advisors then explained the business plan we would all follow.

"Every business is in business to acquire customers," he said. "So, when you think about it, every business plan revolves around numbers. In any business, not everyone who is contacted will purchase a product, whether the business is a brick-and-mortar building, online, or based on cold calls, like ours is. But every business plan is designed around a particular customer, who is called an 'avatar.' An avatar is someone who is a perfect fit for the product or service being sold.

"Now think about this: all business development, no matter the industry, comes down to a numbers game. So, why do we make five hundred calls a day? Because you are all physically capable of doing so. Obviously, there are circumstances that pop up that might limit this number, but, overall, five hundred calls a day is the goal for each and every one of you."

The senior advisor went on to explain that, out of five hundred calls, we would have about one hundred conversations with complete strangers. Of those one hundred calls, two would result in setting up meetings. Of those two meetings, one would be canceled or a no-show. And from those who showed up, one out of four of these meetings would result in a new client(s).

It was simple math. And it was a whole lot easier for me than trying to manage all of the variables when wiring a house or ordering and putting patio furniture together. Every day I told myself, "The more calls I make, the better my opportunities to land clients." So, I was the first one in every day and the last one to leave. While most of my team members were wrapping up early every day, in my mind, there was always time to make one more call before nine o'clock in the evening.

I have always maintained this never-quit-early work ethic. From day one, I knew that the harder I worked, the more clients I would have. To be honest, during the first couple of months, the math didn't work out. But in the third month, something wonderful happened: the math produced way more clients than projected. This led to something even more wonderful. During my first year, I had so many clients to take care of that I had less and less time to make phone calls. My time commitment was changing from client solicitation to client servicing. Math—what a wonderful thing!

As I moved into my third year, people within my office and throughout my district took notice of my success. Maintaining my discipline and work ethic, I was now starting to manage a decent-size portfolio of clients. I was also participating—and continue to do so—in ongoing financial education webinars and seminars, hosted by the world's best fund managers. (I always want to stay current on the continual changes in financial world so that I can give my clients the best direction and guidance.)

In the office, I was considered to be *the* rising star, and team members, new and experienced, started asking if they could join meetings I had with potential and current clients, to see how I worked. They also booked time in my schedule for me to be on their calls with potential clients. What they realized was that I followed a simple methodology that I use to this day: add value to others.

To value someone is to see that person for who they are, including their potential—in this case, their financial potential. I have always genuinely cared for people, and I never tell my clients about my success as a financial advisor. I always focus on how I can best serve them to help each person reach *their* financial goals. I want to fully understand their world so that I can map out a financial plan that best suits my clients.

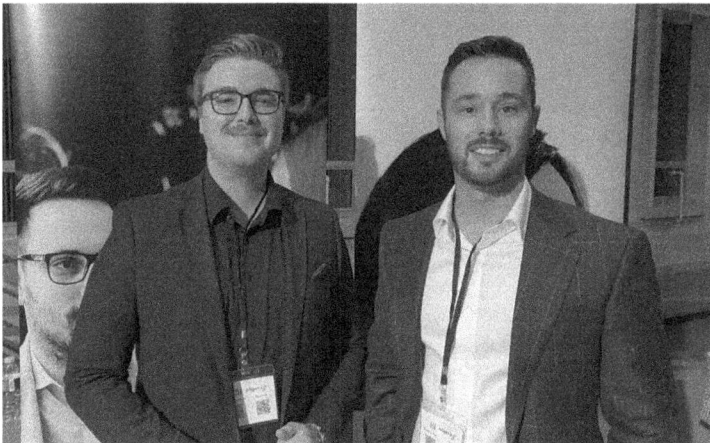

Recruiting event at Laval University, with Nicolas Barriault, Quebec City, 2022. Francis and his team have a long-term partnership with most universities in the province of Quebec, offering financial graduates with the opportunity to start their business in wealth management.

Here's the way my colleagues and I would work together. My colleague would make the cold calls and have the initial conversations. When they had a potential client who wanted to know more, or to meet in person, I would join the meeting to find out more about the individual, their financial goals, or what company managed their investments. I would then brainstorm with my colleague to come up with a plan that we felt was more beneficial to the potential client. If that person decided to transfer their investments over to us to manage, my colleague and I would manage these assets fifty-fifty. This created a win-win-win for everyone. My colleague benefited by gaining a new client and gleaning from my experience. The client benefited by having two investment advisors diligently watching over their investments. And I benefited because I started scaling my business. By "scaling," I mean achieving more with less time.[3] I also realized that scaling my business was equivalent to compounding interest on investments; how sweet is that!

Francis receiving his first award in the finance industry, along with one of his good friends and colleagues, Samuel Briere, who also received an award, 2014.

---

3   Since we all have twenty-four hours in a day and five business days in a week, there is a limit to what we can achieve on our own. Scaling a business means to hire the right people for the right roles to give you more time to work in your area of expertise. If you try to do everything by yourself, you will eventually plateau and stop growing. This principle has led my team and I to manage billions of dollars and help thousands of households building their wealth.

Throughout my career, I've had access to subject matter experts, including senior portfolio managers, fund managers throughout the industry, financial analysts, CPAs, CFAs, lawyers, notaries, and more. The truth is that no single individual—no matter how many degrees they may have or how much experience they have—can be "all things to all people" in the financial world. I was also fortunate enough to start my career with one of the biggest teams in Canada. They were managing billions in assets and had the volume to hire experts throughout the industry, which I had access to. Their expertise, along with my personal studies and research, helped me fast-track the knowledge I needed to become an astute wealth management advisor.

Now that I had found my path in life—a path that encompassed continually helping others reach their financial goals while gaining my own financial independence to live a lifestyle of my own choosing—I wasn't one to rest. Monday to Friday, every morning I continued to be the first one in the office, and throughout the day I would monitor the latest financial and economic news, study funds and charts, and continue to research various financial products and services.

In the evenings, I continue my research and planning for my clients' best interests. I did have an advantage over my colleagues; I only lived ten minutes from my office. In the morning, I would enter the alarm code that told the office managers I was the first one in. In evenings, I would arm the alarm, letting them know I was the last one out. More often than not, I would put in sixteen-hour days, Monday to Thursday, and ten hours on Friday. As well, I would attend financial and investment courses, seminars, and conferences hosted by the best and brightest minds in the investment industry whenever possible. Over the years, I have personally met fund managers and those who run other financial institutions to learn from their experience.

To say that I didn't have much of a social life during the week would be an understatement. But on weekends, I made sure I got extra rest and spent time with friends and family while enjoying life. Enjoying life also included spending a lot of time in the area that I loved the most: motorsports. My passion for motorsports started as a young boy, when I would ride ATVs and dirt bikes at my grandparents' cottage.

I could frequently be found on the racetrack racing cars, along with my friends, or going up north for snowmobiling.

Not surprisingly, as my income grew, a few of my friends grew curious about my business. Over dinner and drinks, or in casual conversations, I would tell them about how I became an investment advisor and my goal to develop my own team. At that time, I realized that if I had a team, I could scale my business, duplicate myself and my knowledge, and help so many more people. It wasn't long before a couple of my friends who had studied finance wanted to join me! After going through the prerequisite training and getting their Canadian securities license, they were at their desks every morning, making their quota of five hundred calls per day.

Francis and family at the Canadian Tire Motorsport Park in Toronto during a racing weekend, summer 2023.

My daily agenda was now full helping all of my colleagues with their clients as well as maintaining a priority on growing clients' portfolios. For example, a client might inherit money, or they might sell a second home. Because I had developed a trusting relationship with my clients, they would ask me to invest their newfound finances. Even today, I continue to scale my business, but I have never reached a place where I am content with the status quo. The internal drive I had as a boy continues to push me forward. And the desire to help others, to serve, to add value, has never left

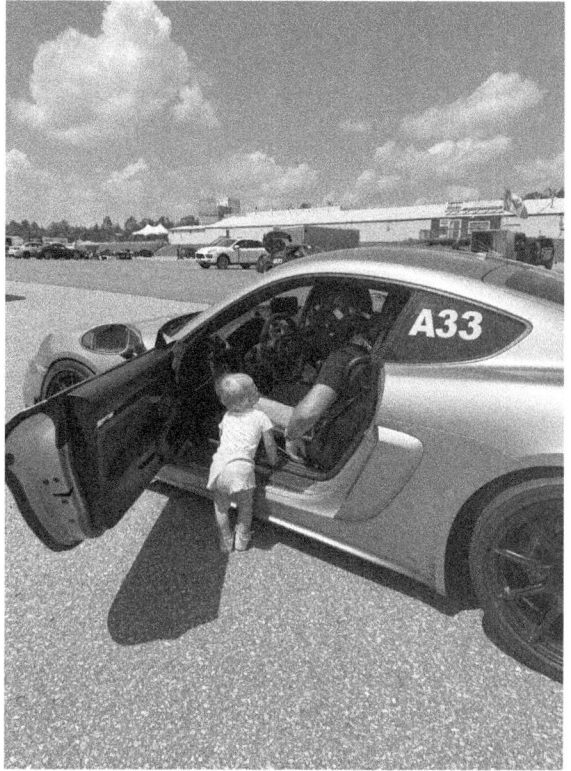

Francis preparing to race at the Canadian Tire Motorsport Park in Toronto, with Sofia helping, summer 2023.

my mind. This includes knowing when a particular client is a better match for one of my team members. As I tell my team over and over, "Always do what is best for the client."

Francis at full speed on the Calabogie Motorsports Park track, summer 2023.

When I first joined the team, I didn't have any preconceived ideas about the position of investment advisor or what the job entailed. But I did have an open mind and was ready for a new career. Even though I was a salesman at my patio furniture store, the idea of "selling" something never appealed to me. When a customer came into the store, I wanted to find out what they were looking for, not what I could sell them. If they had a budget, I stayed within it, instead of trying to talk them into something that would somehow improve their image and lifestyle (which was never the case). I brought this same mindset to my new job.

However, I quickly learned that most financial advisors in the industry were limited to the products and services their institution had to offer. For instance, banks have financial advisors available for their clients, but they can only recommend investments, and other products and services, that the bank provides. In my opinion, only selling in-house investments is a big problem in our industry. I see that as a conflict of interest: Is the advisor doing what is best for the client or what is best for the company? Every financial institution has good and bad products. However, if an advisor is limited to their institution's investments, they cannot go elsewhere to find what is best for the client.

Here's a good analogy. If you walk into a BMW dealership, the representative will tell you how great the car is, and how it is the best fit for you. But if you were also considering a Mercedes, the BMW representative would know very little about that car and may even try to steer you away from a Mercedes.

In my business, we are brokers, and it is our job to be experts in the financial industry, so that we can offer our best advice and guidance to our clients. We do this by getting to know the client and their financial goals and future plans. Then we create a short list of investments and explain how each one works and how it has performed in the past. This allows us to educate our clients on how these investments can help meet their financial goals. All of this gives our clients a comfort level to make informed decisions regarding products that best fit their needs. Does the client want aggressive growth and can they accept the inevitable market ups and downs? Does the client have a more conservative outlook, wanting slower but steady growth for their portfolio? Questions such as these show that each client has their own financial mindset, and it is our job to understand the client and to match investments that align with their goals.

In our position as wealth management advisors, we are all full securities brokers and have access to everything the financial industry has to offer including mutual funds, hedge funds, individual stocks, bonds, exchange-traded funds (ETFs), structured notes,[4] and more. We must earn our money through a direct correlation to the performance of our clients' portfolios. In other words, we are paid a percentage on all of the portfolios we manage, which are called "assets under management." When the market is good, it is our job to grow these assets accordingly, and, to state the obvious, we make a better income. When the markets are in a downturn, we want to protect these same assets, and in doing so, we protect our income as well. For me, this is a great advantage because it appeals to my desire to help others. From day one, I believed this was the right approach to financial investing, and I'm even more convinced today. As the saying goes, "The proof is in the pudding!"

Now that you know more about me, the next two chapters move into your "self-education." First and foremost, it is important to understand your own mindset when it comes to your investing style. My belief is that by understanding yourself, you will understand *why* and *how* you decide on what to invest your hard-earned money in.

TAKEAWAYS

- When you're passionate but unfulfilled, keep asking yourself, "Where is my passion leading me?" You'll find the right path at the right time.

---

4   A structured note is a debt security issued by financial institutions. The return on investment is based on the performance of equity indexes, a single equity, a combination of equities, interest rates, commodities, or foreign currencies.

- Knowledge will tell you who you want to be; hard work will get you where you want to go.

- As I tell my team over and over, "Always do what is best for the client."

- It is the investment advisor's job to understand the client and to match investments that align with their goals.

CHAPTER 5
BEHAVIOURAL INVESTING

The most important quality for an investor
is temperament, not intellect ...

You need a temperament that neither derives great pleasure
from being with the crowd or against the crowd.
—WARREN BUFFETT

W hen I work with my clients, one of the financial terminologies I help them to understand is "behavioural investing." In short, this is a catch-all term used to describe the psychological forces, that is, the emotional drives of the investor, that can have an overwhelming sway on investors' decisions.

For example, consider the following. You are presented with two investment choices: (1) an investment with a fifty-fifty chance of a quick profit and a fifty-fifty chance of a large loss and (2) an investment with a small but long-term profit that also has a lower probability of loss. Which one would you choose?

Most investors would choose investment #2, yet, mathematically, the potential for profit is greater for investment #1. What drives the investor's decision when choosing either investment? The overriding factor is *emotion*. And understanding the effects of emotion is key to understanding behavioural investing.

Whether we realize it or not, we are all driven by our emotions, and when it comes to investing, emotions are a driving force more than we care to admit. For example, someone who is detail oriented and a logical thinker—and considers themselves to be emotionally even keeled—would tend to be a more conservative investor, and investment #2 would fit their mindset. Conversely, a person who is outgoing, enthusiastic, and risk tolerant would be inclined to go with investment #1.

For this reason, I educate my clients on the power that emotions can have when the markets are volatile. When we create a financial plan together, it is with the client's long-term goals in mind. However, I've had clients tell me they want to sell a particular investment that is quickly gaining in value, or they want to hold onto an investment that is losing value. Their reasoning: they don't want to lose what they have gained in the first case, fearing that the investment will reverse course. And in the second case, they are not willing to cut their losses and hold on to the hope that "everything bounces back."

Our emotional makeup isn't something we think about every day, so it is understandable why people deny that their emotions affect their investment decisions. Here are some of the emotional traps that clients can fall into:

- Believing stories that support our emotional outlook and disregarding those that do not. For example, when markets are in a downturn, it's easy to say, "I'm losing money; sell everything!" However, downturns are actually a great time to find solid investments that are now undervalued.

- Having a "herd" mentality. This is chasing after an investment because everyone believes it's the "latest and greatest" or selling an investment because "everyone is doing it."
- Investment paralysis caused by the fear of doing the wrong thing. The truth is that most people lack the financial education to know what the right thing to do is, which is why having an experienced investment advisor is so important.
- Making an investment decision based on how it is presented as opposed to doing factual research.
- Letting the price of an investment determine when to buy, which is akin to trying to "time the market."
- Holding onto a losing investment for too long and selling a "winner" too early. The former is caused by people not wanting to admit making a wrong decision, and the latter is caused by the impatience of wanting to lock in profits too quickly.

The following chart shows how behaviour investment is driven by emotion:[5]

Roller Coaster of Emotion

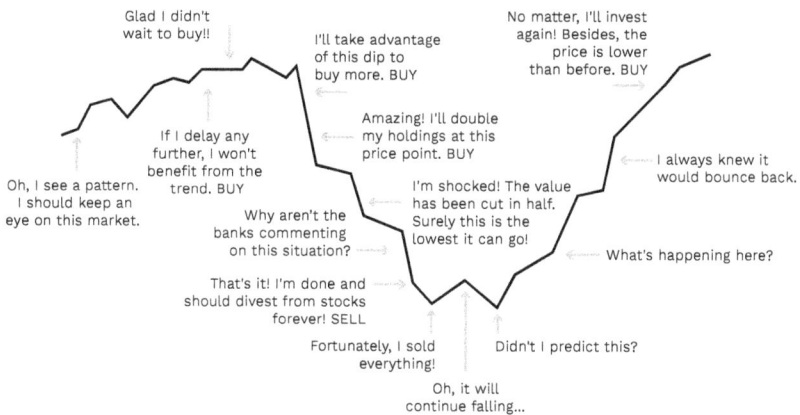

Glad I didn't wait to buy!!

I'll take advantage of this dip to buy more. BUY

No matter, I'll invest again! Besides, the price is lower than before. BUY

If I delay any further, I won't benefit from the trend. BUY

Amazing! I'll double my holdings at this price point. BUY

Oh, I see a pattern. I should keep an eye on this market.

I always knew it would bounce back.

I'm shocked! The value has been cut in half. Surely this is the lowest it can go!

Why aren't the banks commenting on this situation?

What's happening here?

That's it! I'm done and should divest from stocks forever! SELL

Fortunately, I sold everything!

Didn't I predict this?

Oh, it will continue falling...

---

5   Source: Credit Suisse.

Bull versus Bear Markets

As you work with your investment advisor to map out your investment and retirement strategy, you are familiar with the term "bull and bear markets." But what is the difference between these two? To describe how markets are performing:

A bear market occurs when stock prices are falling, the economy is slowing down, and caution is the prevailing mindset. Analysts define a bear market stock prices falling by around 20 percent for a sustained period with the economy characterized by recession, higher unemployment, and reduced consumer spending. A bear market often has a negative impact on corporate profits, with investors having a pessimistic outlook and wanting to sell shares rather than buy them. You may have heard of the dot-com bubble burst in the late 1990s or the financial crisis of 2007–2008, and of course, COVID-19. These were significant factors in creating three of the most recent bear markets.

A bull market happens when the majority of sectors of the economy are growing, unemployment is low, consumer spending rises, and in general, stock prices are rising. Fueled by a growing sense of optimism, investors are buying and/or holding onto assets, creating a buyer's market, which causes stock prices to rise. From the end of the financial crash in 2008 to the start of the pandemic in 2020, the markets have gone through one of the longest bull runs in recorded history.

As the following chart shows, from January 1924 to December 2021, the Canadian stock market has gone through twenty-two bull markets lasting an average of thirty-seven months and twenty-three bear markets lasting an average of fourteen months:

Bull vs. Bear Market

CANADIAN EQUITY
January 1924 – December 2021

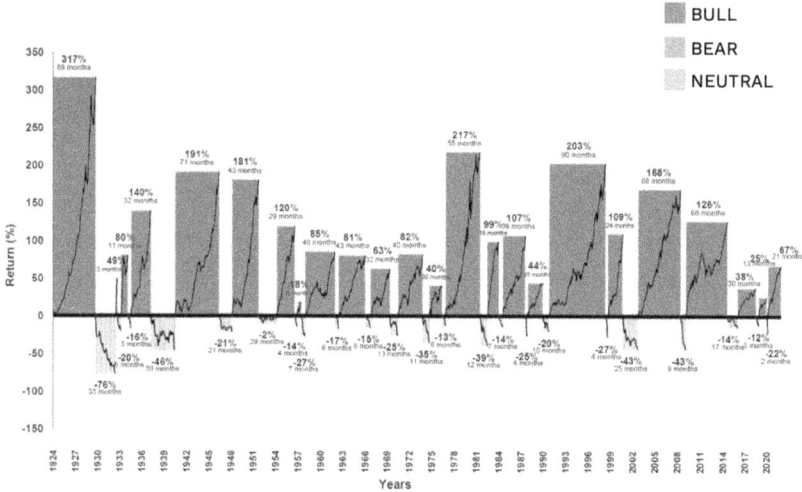

BULL AND BEAR FACTS

Average gain in bull markets: +110%   Average loss in bear markets: -34%

Average length of bull markets: 37 months   Average length of bear markets: 14 months

"Bull vs. Bear Market in Canadian Stocks, 1924 to 2021 – Chart," Top Foreign Stocks, September 26, 2022, accessed October 9, 2022, https://topforeignstocks. com/2022/09/26/bull-vs-bear-market-in-canadian-stocks-1924-to-2021-chart/.

Note: Returns represent past performance, are not a guarantee of future performance, and are not indicative of any specific investment.

In the United States, equity markets have gone through ten unique bear markets in the past seventy years, which suggests investors can expect to encounter a bear market approximately once every seven years:

A History of U.S. Equity of Bull & Bear Markets

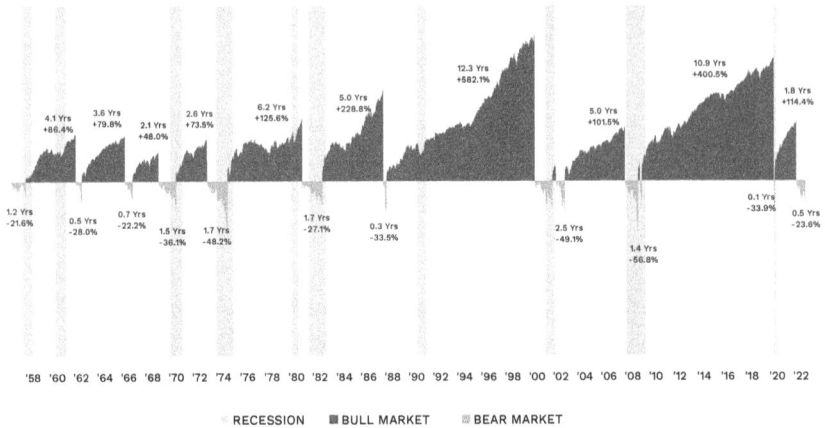

"S&P 500 Index Bull and Bear Markets," chart, RBC Global Asset Management, data from Bloomberg, June 13, 2022, accessed April 15, 2024, https://www.rbcgam. com/en/ca/learn-plan/investment-basics/the-bulls-the-bears/detail.

Note: An investment cannot be made directly into an index. The graph does not reflect transaction costs, investment management fees, or taxes. If such costs and fees were reflected, returns would be lower. Past performance is not a guarantee of future results. Bull market starts from lowest close reached after the market has fallen 20 percent or more. Bear market starts from when the index closes at least 20 percent down from its previous high.

What Does All of This Mean?

Behavioural investing often leads to bad market timing when buying or selling an asset. While the media can be a good source of determining when bull or bear markets are evolving, the media can also be the source of creating an emotional "buzz" that can be outdated, short-lived, or even hearsay and based on rumors.

No matter what type of market the economy is in, behaviour investing comes into play as the following chart shows:

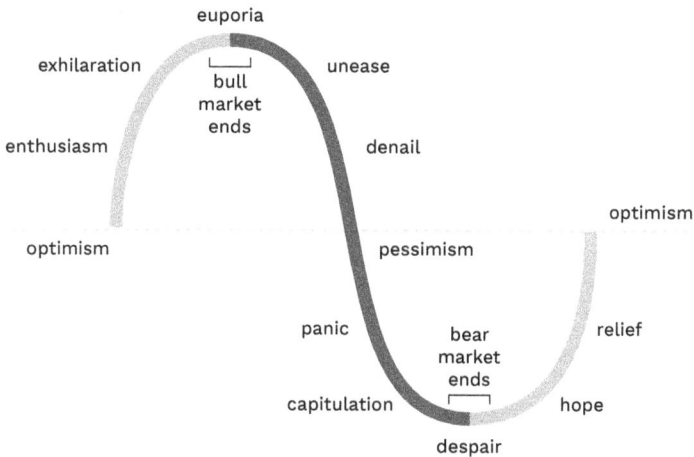

euporia

exhilaration — bull market ends — unease

enthusiasm — denial

optimism

optimism — pessimism

panic — bear market ends — relief

capitulation — hope

despair

Barry Ritholtz, "Psychology Charts & Sentiment Cycles (updated)," The Big Picture, March 24, 2014, last modified March 24, 2014, accessed December 12, 2022, https://ritholtz.com/2014/03/psychology-charts-sentiment-cycles-updated/.

An astute wealth management advisor can help their clients use rational and realistic thinking to understand their financial goals and to follow the plan created to achieve these goals. Reacting to the latest breaking economic news indicates that decisions are being driven by emotion rather than logic and rationale.

Strategies to Eliminate Emotion When Investing

The wisest strategies for your investment planning are best determined through conversations with your investment advisor. However, before doing so, it is important to understand the most common investment strategies. Here are eight of the most popular investment strategies:

1. BUY AND HOLD

Buy and hold is the most commonly used strategy for long-term goals. In simple terms, an asset is bought and held until financial goals are reached and the investor's financial plan shifts. For example, if a stock or fund is purchased and held for, say, tenyears, once the investor moves from their career into retirement, money made could then be used to fund travel, purchase a condo, or whatever needs the investor has at that time. How well a buy-and-hold portfolio performs is dependent upon the assets that are held.

A key to this type of strategy is that individual investors can be their own worst enemies and too often sell their investments at the wrong time. A buy-and-hold strategy eliminates that problem. Buy-and-hold assets are companies that have been or are likely to be around for a long time. These are companies with strong brands that you recognize in your daily life. Keep your positions small so that any stock that devalues will not greatly affect your portfolio and those that do well boost your portfolio.

The following chart is an example showing the importance of maintaining a buy-and-hold strategy:

Keeping a Long-Term View
DESPITE SETBACKS, THE S&P/TSX COMPOSITE TOTAL RETURN INDEXSHOWS GROWTH OVER THE LONG TERM

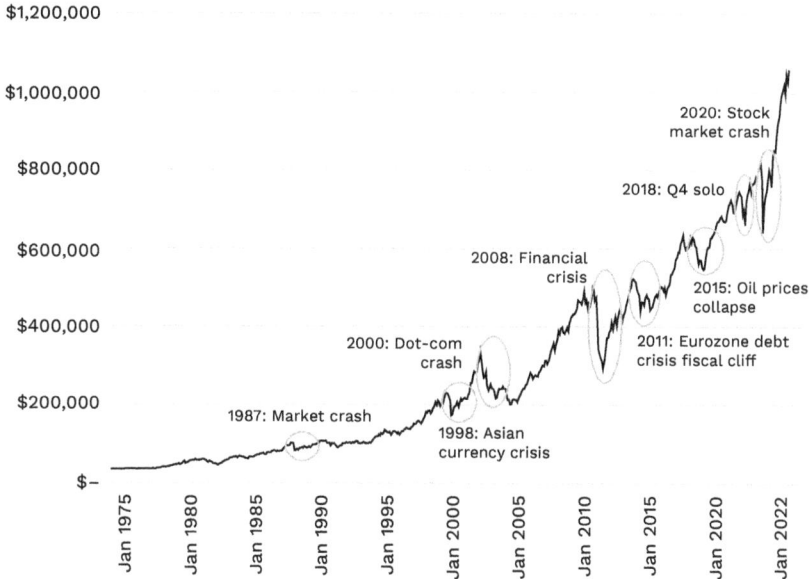

"S&P/TSX Composite Total Return Index, January 1, 1975-December 31, 2021,"
Chart, Morningstar, accessed April 15, 2024.

Note: For illustration purposes only. The circles indicate periods of market decline. Past performance is not indicative of future performance. S&P/TSX Composite Total Return Index. The index is unmanaged and cannot be purchased directly by investors.

2. GROWTH INVESTING

A growth investment strategy gives you the opportunity to invest in the fastest growing sectors and industries capable of producing high annual returns. Researching sectors and companies presents the opportunity to learn about who is innovating and creating the future. However, while growth stocks typically have the highest valuations in the market, investing should be done with caution. Companies need to develop a track record and live up to expectations to justify their valuations. If not, the stock price will correct, quickly and dramatically. Research must win over market opinion.

3. VALUE INVESTING

Value investing focuses on companies with solid earning that trade at or below their fair market value. Consider that this type of investing has produced the most consistent long-term returns over the last one hundred years, and the most well-known investor in the world, Warren Buffett, has made much of his fortune this way. It is important for investors' financial statements to determine the true value of a company in order to identify the high-quality stocks that are discounted.

4. SMALL CAP INVESTING

Small cap investing focuses on companies valued between $300 million and $2 billion. It is easier for these companies to double their value compared with mid- or large-market cap companies, but they can be overlooked by investors and there are two main advantages to focusing on smaller companies. First, it is easier for a small company to grow its profits. Doubling revenue from a base level of $100 million is a lot easier than to trade it at a discount. However, they are less likely to be liquid—they can be harder to sell—and their share price can be more volatile.

5. DIVIDEND INVESTING

Dividend investing, also known as income investing or yield investing, focuses on generating a steady stream of income. High dividends can be found with very profitable stocks, but they also have slow rates of growth. Wise investors will reinvest their dividends as a way to grow their portfolio without using their own money. Companies that pay dividends tend to be quite profitable, making dividend investing a good strategy during times of recession.

6. DOLLAR COST AVERAGING

With this strategy, set amounts are invested at regular and predetermined intervals. Dollar cost averaging can be used in any market condition, eliminating the guesswork out of trying to time a market. When the market is trending down, shares are purchased at a lower price, which balances out higher-priced shares purchased when the market is trending up. One of the great advantages of this strategy is that lower-priced shares produce greater capital gains when markets are positive. The key to this strategy is to maintain regular purchases.

7. DIVERSIFICATION

As the name of this strategy states, diversification is about purchasing a variety of investments rather than just one or two assets. Diversification helps to diminish emotional responses to market volatility by providing protection. Rarely do all industries move in unison, and a diversified portfolio takes into account different industries and sectors and can even include real estate and private equity, as the following chart shows:

2006	2007	2008	2009	2010	2011	2012	2013	2014	2015	2016	2017	2018	2019	2020	2021	2022
11.8%[9]	9.5%[1]	13.7%[3]	57.5%[9]	15.2%[9]	9.8%[3]	18.5%[11]	7.4%[9]	8.8%[7]	3.7%[8]	17.5%[9]	9.3%[11]	2.4%[8]	14.4%[11]	9.4%[4]	5.4%[9]	-0.6%[6]
9.9%[11]	9.0%[3]	11.5%[8]	51.6%[6]	12.0%[11]	9.7%[7]	15.6%[9]	5.3%[6]	7.6%[5]	3.5%[7]	10.2%[11]	7.5%[9]	1.9%[11]	14.4%[5]	9.2%[1]	5.2%[6]	-4.0%[10]
6.7%[6]	7.0%[2]	8.6%[10]	28.2%[11]	10.1%[6]	8.5%[11]	9.7%[6]	1.7%[10]	7.5%[4]	2.7%[5]	10.2%[6]	7.4%[6]	1.4%[7]	13.8%[4]	8.7%[5]	-0.9%[10]	-9.34%[8]
6.6%[1]	6.3%[11]	6.4%[7]	16.3%[5]	8.5%[4]	8.4%[8]	9.4%[4]	0.8%[5]	6.9%[8]	2.6%[10]	5.6%[4]	6.2%[4]	1.1%[5]	8.7%[2]	8.7%[7]	-1.1%[4]	-9.87%[5]
4.4%[5]	5.1%[4]	5.2%[2]	16.0%[4]	7.3%[5]	8.4%[4]	6.2%[5]	-1.2%[7]	6.0%[2]	1.2%[11]	3.7%[5]	4.1%[1]	0.9%[3]	8.6%[3]	8.0%[3]	-1.3%[5]	-11.2%[9]
4.3%[4]	4.6%[8]	4.8%[1]	6.9%[1]	6.7%[7]	8.2%[5]	4.3%[1]	-1.5%[8]	5.5%[11]	0.8%[3]	2.6%[2]	3.5%[2]	0.4%[6]	8.1%[6]	7.5%[2]	-1.5%[11]	-11.7%[7]
4.3%[2]	4.1%[10]	0.2%[5]	5.9%[2]	6.5%[2]	7.8%[2]	4.2%[2]	-2.0%[4]	5.1%[3]	0.5%[2]	2.1%[1]	3.4%[5]	0.0%[2]	6.9%[7]	7.3%[8]	-1.5%[2]	-12.5%[3]
4.1%[7]	3.7%[7]	-3.1%[4]	5.4%[7]	5.9%[3]	5.6%[1]	3.6%[7]	-2.0%[2]	3.1%[10]	-0.7%[6]	1.7%[7]	2.5%[7]	-1.2%[1]	6.9%[9]	6.2%[9]	-2.3%[3]	-13.0%[2]
4.0%[10]	2.2%[9]	-10.9%[11]	4.5%[10]	5.5%[1]	4.7%[10]	2.1%[8]	-2.6%[1]	2.5%[9]	-0.8%[4]	1.0%[3]	2.3%[3]	-2.1%[4]	6.8%[1]	5.9%[11]	-2.5%[7]	-15.3%[4]
3.6%[8]	2.1%[6]	-26.4%[9]	-0.2%[8]	5.4%[8]	4.4%[9]	2.0%[10]	-2.7%[3]	1.6%[6]	-3.2%[1]	1.0%[10]	0.1%[8]	-2.3%[9]	3.7%[8]	5.3%[10]	-2.6%[8]	-16.2%[1]
3.1%[3]	1.8%[5]	-29.1%[6]	-3.6%[3]	3.6%[10]	1.5%[6]	2.0%[3]	-6.6%[11]	0.6%[1]	-4.6%[9]	0.0%[8]	0.1%[10]	-4.6%[10]	3.1%[10]	3.1%[6]	-4.7%[1]	-16.5%[11]

FIXED INCOME ASSET CLASSES

[1] Global Bonds	[2] US Aggregate	[3] US Treasury	[4] US Credit
[5] Canadian Corporate Bonds	[6] US Floating Rate	[7] Canadian Bond Universe	[8] Canadian Government Bonds
[9] US High Yield Bonds	[10] Canadian Short Term Bonds	[11] Emerging Market Debt	

Source: As of September 30, 2022. Floating Rate (S&P/LSTA Leveraged Loan Index), Canada Bond Universe (DEX Universe Bond), Canada Inv. Corporate Bonds (DEX Corporate Bond), Canadian Government Bond (DEX Federal Universe Bond), Canadian Short Term Bonds (DEX Short Term Bond), Global Blonds (Barclays Global Aggregate), US High Yield (BofA ML US High Yield Master II Unconstrained), Emerging Market Debt (JPM EMBI Global)

Manulife Investment Management, Capital Markets Strategy, "Various fixed income asset class annual yearly returns," Bloomberg, December 31, 2022, accessed January 6, 2023.

8. CONTRARIAN INVESTING

A contrarian is someone who goes against prevailing market sentiments. Contrarian investing means investing in assets that go against what others are doing. When the stock market is trending down, contrarian investors are buying, and when markets are trending up, these investors are selling. In other words, they go against the herd mentality. For example, much of Warren Buffett's approach to investing is contrarian. He looks for stocks that are out of favor and are closely examined for their fundamentals and value. As a contrarian, he is quoted as famously saying, "I will tell you how to become rich. Close the doors. Be fearful when others are greedy. Be greedy when others are fearful."

"You" Are the Single Most Important Factor

No matter what type of investment style you choose, "you" are the single most important factor. You might be saying, "That's obvious. It's my money, so I get to choose when, where, and how to invest." However, what I'm talking about is your *temperament*. Temperament is the way you are hardwired to make decisions and determines your outlook on life, and in this case, finances. Are you a risk-taker? Someone who is conservative with your money? Do you tend to worry or take things as they come? These outlooks are based on your temperament. And your temperament will determine your behavioural investing philosophy. While there are many types of temperament

No matter what type of investment style you choose, "you" are the single most important factor.

assessments, the four most common temperaments are choleric, sanguine, melancholic, and phlegmatic. The following shows how each of these relates to behavioural investment.

Choleric individuals tend to be shrewd, analytical, and logical. They are also practical and straightforward. Retail investor specialist Richard Harmon calls these investors the "Controlled Risk-Taker":[6]

> This type of investor wants to make all the money when the general market goes up but wants to lose very little during drawdowns. Much of their investment portfolio is in equity positions. These investors are typically well informed on what the general market is doing. Buy and hold won't work during periods of large drawdowns, so they employ active management in bad times. They will quickly reduce portfolio equity exposure at early signs of emotional pain.

People who are *sanguines* are energetic, optimistic, flexible, and light-hearted. They look for adventure and have high risk tolerance. Harmon labels these investors as the "risk seeker":[7]

> This type of investor wants to make as much money as possible, regardless of risk. This type wants to make at least as much as the general stock market going up. On the way down they aren't happy, but they won't sell, knowing they will make back their portfolio losses and then some in the future. They are extremely confident individuals. A spin-off of the risk seeker is one that has the same objective, however their reaction during large drawdowns is different. They start to panic, even though they came in with a long-term game

---

6   Robert Harmon, "Know Yourself: The Four Temperament Investments," December 18, 2018, https://investspectrum.com/uma/tag/temperament/.

7   Ibid.

plan. They know the risks involved with investing aggressively, but eventually they will sell everything at the worst possible time.

Individuals with *melancholic* temperaments love anything that is traditional. They love family and friends and want to maintain the status quo in their lives. Harmon calls these investors the "Preservationist":[8]

> This type of investor wants to make money with much less risk than the stock market. They feel safer with bonds because they aren't as volatile. Many investors with this mentality either fear they will run out of money in their retirement years, or they want to give it all to their children/grandchildren. They simply want to be reassured that their principal is still there. Any growth is a positive.

Finally, people with a *phlegmatic* temperament desire harmony within themselves and strive to keep close relationships. They are loyal to their friends, family, and spouses and want to maintain relationships for as long as possible. Harmon classifies these investors as the "Balancer":[9]

> This type of investor wants to make money in line with stock market returns, but they want downside protection. They know stocks are riskier than bonds and the next bear market will eventually come. They like being in a diversified stock/bond/alternative portfolio.

As you can see, understanding who you are has a direct effect on how you invest. When you know yourself, you can choose an invest-

---

8   Ibid.

9   Ibid.

ment strategy that fits who you are, which will then determine your behavioural investment philosophy.

TAKEAWAYS

- Whether we realize it or not, we are all driven by our emotions, and when it comes to investing, emotions are a driving force more than we care to admit.

- Analysts define a *bear market* stock prices falling by around 20 percent for a sustained period with the economy characterized by recession, higher unemployment, and reduced consumer spending.

- A bull market happens when the majority of sectors of the economy are growing, unemployment is low, consumer spending rises, and in general, stock prices are rising.

- There are many different types of investment strategies. However, your temperament will determine your overall investment philosophy, so it is important to understand yourself *first* before determining how and what you want to invest in.

Personal Takeaways

WHAT DID I LEARN? WHAT ARE MY FUTURE STEPS?

CHAPTER 6

COMMON RISKS TO RETIREMENT INVESTING AND FINANCIAL FREEDOM

While enthusiasm may be necessary for great accomplishments elsewhere, on Wall Street it almost invariably leads to disaster.
—BENJAMIN GRAHAM

No matter what stage of financial planning you are in, it is important to be aware of and understand the common risks to your retirement plan and financial stability. The *Toronto Star* published the following chart showing reasons why Canadians delay their retirement:

Inflation Delays Retirement for Half of Older Canadians

RESULTS OF A SURVEY OF CANADIANS OLDER THAN 55 CONDUCTED IN JUNE 2022.

I have delayed (or plan to delay) my retirement because...

I don't have enough savings/investments	**62%**
Rising inflation/cost of living this year	**54%**

I have too much debt	**40%**
My children still require financial support	**26%**
I love my job too much to quit	**23%**
The COVID-19 pandemic	**21%**
I am taking care of my partner/spouse	**13%**
I am taking care of a parent or other family member	**10%**

"How Can I Protect My Retirement Nest Egg against Inflation?" Toronto Star, October 3, 2022, https://www.thestar.com/business/personal_finance/2022/10/03/how-can-i-protect-my-retirement-nest-egg-against-inflation.html.

The goal of this chapter is education, which, in my mind, is key to eliminating fear of the future. So, let's look at some of these risks and what can be done to plan for each one.

Lifestyle Inflation

When people think of the word "inflation," they naturally recognize it as an economic term. Inflation affects all aspects of our economy, and we'll talk about this shortly. However, lifestyle inflation is just as important to discuss. Think about this. You have been working for a particular company for several years, and you just got hired by another business that pays you a lot more; in fact, your take-home pay has increased 30 percent overnight. The first thing you do is think of how you are going to *spend* that extra money: a new car, a larger home or apartment, a vacation, new clothes—the list is endless.

Lifestyle inflation is a simple equation that most people follow: The more you earn, the more you spend. It is termed "lifestyle inflation" because one's standard of living goes up in relation to the income earned. The problem is that people tend to spend like there is no tomorrow instead of saving *for* tomorrow. And in doing so, they shortchange their financial future. For example, if you were to spend $500 of extra pay from your new job, you could cost yourself literally years of extra work. Consider that investing $500/month over ten years at an annualized 5 percent rate of return would net an extra $75,000.

Lifestyle inflation is a simple equation that most people follow.

The main problem associated with lifestyle inflation is that once spending habits are formed, they are hard to break or change. Our economy is debt-driven, meaning that people borrowing money to support their lifestyle is the driving force. Lifestyle deflation that includes cutting back on spending, and developing a regular habit of saving and investing, is not something most people are excited about. Let me be clear that I'm not against anyone enjoying what they earn. After all, a save-save-save mentality is what got Charles Dickens's immortal character, Scrooge, into trouble. But a constant mindset of "I deserve this" will never prepare anyone for a secure financial future. The adage, "Sacrifice today for a brighter tomorrow," is a good way to curb lifestyle inflation. Here are four easy ways to combat lifestyle inflation:

1. Create a budget and stick to it by tracking your spending closely.
2. Pay down debt as fast as possible.
3. Eliminate credit card spending, or when needed, use cash-back credit cards.
4. Use coupons whenever possible and discount websites.

Economic Inflation

Let's say that you are committed to planning for your retirement and future financial stability. In this case, economic inflation must be taken into account. Inflation itself is much like the wind: you can feel its effects, but you cannot see it nor do you know when it is coming or going. Consider the following chart from the Canadian Financial Consumer Agency:

Inflation is the rising cost of consumer goods. It affects your retirement needs in two ways.

First, the cost of the goods that you buy increases. Over twenty-five years, an inflation rate of 2.5 percent nearly doubles the cost of the goods you buy, as this chart shows.

Cost of goods at an annual inflation rate of 2.5%

NUMBER OF YEARS	IF YOUR ANNUAL EXPENSES ARE $20,000	IF YOUR ANNUAL EXPENSES ARE $40,000
1	$20,500	$41,000
5	$22,628	$45,256
15	$28,966	$57,932
25	$37,079	$74,158

Financial Consumer Agency of Canada, "Investing and Registered Retirement Savings Plans (RRSPs)," Government of Canada, last modified March 17, 2023, accessed April 15, 2024, https://www.canada.ca/en/financial-consumer-agency/services/financial-toolkit/retirement-pensions/retirement-pensions-1/8.html.

Second, it means that your savings lose value. Over twenty-five years, with an inflation rate of 2.5 percent, your savings lose nearly half of their value, as this chart shows. (This does not take into account the return on your investments—that is, the profit you make on any savings you invest.)

Value of savings at an annual inflation rate of 2.5%

NUMBER OF YEARS	IF YOUR SAVINGS TOTAL $20,000	IF YOUR SAVINGS TOTAL $40,000
1	$19,512	$39,024
5	$17,677	$35,354
15	$13,809	$27,619
25	$10,788	$21,576

Financial Consumer Agency of Canada, "Investing and Registered Retirement Savings Plans (RRSPs)," Government of Canada, last modified March 17, 2023, accessed April 15, 2024, https://www.canada.ca/en/financial-consumer-agency/services/financial-toolkit/retirement-pensions/retirement-pensions-1/8.html.

With inflation both increasing the cost of the goods you buy and decreasing the value of your savings, you will need more money to maintain the same level of purchasing power over time. Take the rate of inflation into account when you project how much money you will need to cover your retirement years.

Inflation is measured with a tool called the Canadian Consumer Price Index. Statistics Canada compares year-over-year pricing on a range of products and services, such as food, housing, and transportation to determine this index. The Bank of Canada then uses its "key interest rate"—the rate the Bank of Canada charges banks to borrow money when they fall short of their required reserves—to influence the economy. Historically, the bank tries to regulate inflation to 2 percent per year.

There are three "legs" to Canada's retirement income system, the first two of which are indexed to the cost of living, meaning they pay a little more each year to help compensate for inflation: (1) Old Age Security (OAS) and the Guaranteed Income Supplement (GIS); (2) Canada Pension Plan (CPP), which covers virtually all employed and self-employed people in Canada, excluding Quebec, which operates its own comprehensive Quebec Pension Plan; and (3) private savings and investments.

Living Too Long

Certainly, living a long and full life is the goal of every Canadian. However, the most often asked question of any investment advisor is, "Am I going to run out of money?" The answer is no, because of federal and provincial plans that provide an income. However, what people are really asking is, "Can I afford my lifestyle throughout my lifetime?" To answer this question, it is critical to do a cash flow analysis to understand future goals and the income needed to support those goals. Cash flow analysis includes projected income and debt and factors in products such as life and disability insurance.

Dying Too Soon

We all know the stark reality that death is part of life, and making sure that financial investments are accessible to your loved ones through joint accounts or having a will is foundational to securing their financial future. Life insurance is also a major factor in relieving any financial burdens because of premature death. Keep in mind that reduced government spousal plan payments must also be accounted for.

The Most Common Types of Life Insurance

PERMANENT LIFE INSURANCE	TERM LIFE INSURANCE
WHAT?	**WHAT?**
■ Permanent life insurance is the right choice for individuals wanting a lifelong death benefit, the ability to use their policy in retirement, and the potential to build tax-deferred cash value over time.	■ Term life insurance offers financial protection from over fixed time periods—usually 5 to 30 years, for a low, fixed cost.
■ This policy can cover final expenses, supplement retirement income, pay off debt, or fund other long-term goals.	■ A company will to pay the death benefit in exchange for on-time premium payments. If the policy holder dies before the term is over, their beneficiary receives the death benefit in a tax-free lump sum. If the policy holder is alive when the term ends, they can: cancel the policy if the coverage is no longer need; renew the policy at their current age; convert part or all of the death benefit to a permanent policy, like whole or universal life
WHO?	
■ It is convenient for individuals wanting a simple approach to covering inevitable expenses that will be incurred at some point during their life.	
■ While the policy tends to be more expensive, the premiums stay consistent, making the policy easy to budgeting purposes.	**WHO?**
	■ For those looking for value and affordability, or for temporary coverage that fits into their financial plan

Becoming Critically Ill or Disabled

Every day we wake up and think, "Nothing is going to happen to me today." Yet, consider that "[r]esearchers estimated that there would be 233,900 new cancer cases and 85,100 cancer deaths in Canada in 2022."[10] And that's just from one disease! Transport Canada reported that in 2020, there were 1,745 fatalities and 7,868 serious injuries reported from car accidents.[11]

Statistically, Canadians are far more likely to get sick or injured than to die too soon. This shows the importance of having critical illness and/or disability insurance as part of a solid financial plan. The average cost for a disability insurance policy is 2 percent, and critical illness policies can be structured with different features and with term limits or level cost for life, so the question to ask is: Would you rather

---

10 "Cancer Statistics at a Glance," Canadian Cancer Society, https://cancer.ca/en/research/cancer-statistics/cancer-statistics-at-a-glance.

11 "Canadian Motor Vehicle Traffic Collision Statistics: 2020," https://tc.canada.ca/en/road-transportation/statistics-data/canadian-motor-vehicle-traffic-collision-statistics-2020.

get paid 98 percent of what you earn today and ensure you continue to receive that income in the event of a disability? Or are you a gambler and willing to bet that you won't get sick or disabled?

In the next chapter, I will go back to my own financial and investment philosophy so that you have a deeper understanding of how I help my clients.

TAKEAWAYS

- With the right financial plan in place, your retirement doesn't need to be delayed, unless you want to.

- The main problem associated with lifestyle inflation is that once spending habits are formed, they are hard to break or change.

- It is critical to do a cash flow analysis to understand future goals and the income needed to support your goals. Cash flow analysis includes projected income and debt, and factors in products such as life and disability insurance.

- Having the right type of insurance policy, or policies, in place is critical for your life and for your beneficiaries.

Personal Takeaways

WHAT DID I LEARN? WHAT ARE MY FUTURE STEPS?

_____

_____

_____

_____

_____

_____

_____

_____

_____

_____

_____

_____

_____

_____

_____

_____

_____

_____

_____

_____

_____

_____

_____

_____

CHAPTER 7

ADDING VALUE TO OTHERS

Adding value to others is the surest
way to add to our own lives.
—JOHN C. MAXWELL

Enjoying life comes in different ways to different people. In my case, I enjoy working over relaxing. Don't get me wrong, I wouldn't call myself a workaholic; I truly enjoy what I do! And the big reason is that I can add value to others—I can help them achieve their financial goals so that they can live the type of lifestyle they want to live.

This mindset plays out at my home as well. I have always had the mindset that whomever I would spend my life with would not have to work, if she chose not to. Audrey Ann, my fiancée, has that luxury; she can choose to work, to volunteer at a charity, or whatever else she decides to do. And it's so great to see she loves and cares for our daughters, Sofia and Olivia, and takes great care of me as well, so we are "adding value" to each other's lives.

Money is simply a tool and one that is always in abundance—that is, if you have the right mindset and understand how to grow the money you have. For example, I believe that generosity returns generosity. If you are generous with your time, money, and resources and if you're generous with the love and care that you share, these will come back to you in increased measure.

I also believe that money is an unlimited resource. In the right hands and with the right mindset, money can and will compound, meaning that it has unlimited potential to grow. The problem as I see it is that people get attached to money, meaning they have a me-first mentality. But money is meant for more than just meeting the basics in life. While I'm not a religious person, there is a verse in the Bible that says your heart follows your treasure.[12] That leads to a question that I often ask myself, "Do I have money or does money have me?"

When it comes to making money and achieving financial independence, I see endless possibilities. I think we are all capable of making the type of income we want; it comes down to what we are willing to do, legally, morally, and ethically, to make that income. What are we willing to sacrifice today to get what we need in the future? For instance, you may know people who attend college or university classes in the evenings and on weekends, so they can earn a degree that leads to a promotion. You may know others who are starting a home-based business or using their current skills to earn extra income.

I truly believe that our income is limited by our mindset because income is only a belief. For instance, someone earning $100,000 a year will never make much more than this unless they unlock the possibilities in their mind.

---

12   The Bible, English Standard Version, accessed April 15, 2024, https://www.biblegate-way.com/passage/?search=Matthew+6%3A21&version=ESV.

One way to do this is to continually ask yourself, "What if?" That question allows you to begin to see beyond your current realities and to begin to explore your potential and the potential in situations that present themselves. I believe that we all have a blueprint of our ideal life sitting in our subconscious mind. The income you earn today is only a reflection of what you think your time is worth financially. The good news is that you can add zeros to any number, and ten times your income, when you start by changing what you believe you are entitled to. I have always worked very hard all my life, but my income never grew because of hard work; it grew whenever my mindset changed.

I learned that if I hang out with people making $100,000 a year, I will probably end up making the same. But as I changed the circle of people around me, their financial mindsets, philosophies, and their approach to money started rubbing off on me, and I now have the same financial freedom that they have.

When I'm helping a client to plan their financial future, I do my best to help them see and understand that their finances aren't limited to their current situation. For instance, if you start hanging out with people making a million per year, you will probably end up there yourself. Same thing applies to having a $10M income a year. I help my clients to understand that adding zeros to their income starts in the mind. The saying, "See yourself there before you get there," applies. I'm of the belief—and my life is proof—that having this mindset has worked over and over for me.

Money is no different from anything else in the way it creates reality; whatever we see and have in our physical world today was once only in our collective imagination. You have to see it in your mind to hold it in your hands. This might all sound crazy but there is a science behind the correlation between what you see in your mind and what becomes reality in your life. This correlation happens in the "theta waves" within the brain. Theta waves naturally happen twice a day; when you are just waking up but your eyes are still closed and when you are in the process of falling asleep.[13]

I have also found that theta waves can be created through visualization. Visualization is a way of focusing your mind to consciously imagine the reality that you wish to materialize. For example, if you are preparing for a job interview, you can visualize going through the interview and nailing it, then being offered the job. Athletes do the same thing. Before their game or event, they visualize themselves competing and winning. This will tap into the brain's theta waves, allowing you to "see" the outcome that you want before the actual event occurs. As a side note, visualization gives you access to your subconscious mind. We live 95 percent of our lives through our subconscious mind, and only 5 percent of our consciousness is solicited daily.[14] Therefore, it is crucial to change our mindsets on a subconscious level in order to affect our beliefs and behaviours.[15]

While I didn't know it at the time, the phrase "adding value to others" has appealed to me ever since I was a kid. As I have noted, while other kids my age were riding bikes and having fun, I was focused on earning money. But I wasn't earning money for the sake of it; I genuinely knew that if I was financially independent, then I could help people from all walks of life.

---

13   "Theta Waves in Psychology | Definition & Benefits," https://study.com/academy/ lesson/theta-waves-psychology-overview-hertz-benefits.html.

14   "ENGL 2210 World Literature II," http://webhome.auburn.edu/~mitrege/ENGL2210/ USNWR-mind.html.

15   There are a lot of good books on the topics of visualization and the conscious and subconscious mind. Personally, I love the work of Dr. Joe Dispenza and have learned a lot from him.

As an investment advisor, adding value to my clients is first and foremost in my mind.

To be honest, I think there is a hypocritical side to the financial industry in general. What I mean is, every financial institution will tell you they want to add value to their clients' lives. But if you think about it, most of these same financial institutions are publicly traded companies. As such, the

We live 95 percent of our lives through our subconscious mind, and only 5 percent of our consciousness is solicited daily.

company's focus is on their shareholders; how can the company increase shareholder profits? This means that what is in the best interest of the shareholder may not necessarily be in the best interest of the individual client. Shareholders want a return on their investment, and one way to do this is to sell high-end products that aren't necessarily the best for each client but will increase company profits. Giving the best return possible to the shareholder means continually increasing sales. When you increase the sales, the client is being charged more. I see this as a direct contradiction.

I believe that adding value to my clients means researching the best investments possible for each client, based on their goals and objectives. Everyone has different goals. Everyone has different risk tolerances. Everyone has different timelines.

As brokers, we have access to investment products and services throughout the industry. I also have access to lawyers, accountants, and a host of other experts ready to help my clients. The ability to add value to others is why I am so passionate about what I do. I don't see what I am doing as a "job" per se; I see it as my life's path, and I have strong convictions about "doing the right thing because it's the right thing to do" as a friend of mine says.

The fact that our pay is linked directly to the performance of our client's portfolios eliminates any conflict of interest, in my opinion. I am able to shop around, to compare different funds, to analyze funds and stocks, to talk to money managers throughout the industry. This allows me to educate my clients and give guidance and direction as to what I feel is best for them but leaving final decisions up to each client. If my firm had their own specific investment products, and I was limited to telling my clients about these only, how would I be adding value to each client?

As an investment advisor, I am determined to leave "no stone unturned" in order to find out what is in my clients' best interest. Understanding my clients' goals for their current life and retirement allows us to plan together for today and the future. What does retirement look like in financial terms? How much income is needed on a yearly, monthly, or weekly basis, taking into account inflation and other factors? How much does the client need to invest today, whether weekly, monthly, yearly, or a lump sum, and what rate of return is needed in order to achieve their goals? How early can they start to invest in order to retire at the age they want to? And if something should happen to the client, and they were no longer alive to provide for their family, what does estate planning look like, in order to keep as much money in the estate as possible and limit estate taxes. Also, questions regarding life insurance, disability insurance, critical illness insurance, paying down any loans or mortgages, and managing a budget need to be addressed. Including all of these in my discussions with my clients means taking time to get to know each client individually.

I recently had the chance to speak to many individuals within my industry who have similar job descriptions as mine. Our discussions inevitably lead to a comparison of companies that we are working for. For many of these people, when I explain that I have almost unlimited research, an abundance of experts, and financial products and services from across the industry at my disposal, these same people can see how limited they are. They see the limitations they have in truly helping their clients achieve their financial goals and, in return, increasing their own compensation.

Conversations such as these are especially helpful to young professionals who have been recruited after graduation to work for a particular financial institution. Being young, these people think there is only one path they can take as an investment advisor. Granted, they start out with a good salary, which will increase over the years. But salaries, by nature, are always limited. However, when I explain that working with us is like having your own business, with your own client base, with an unlimited income ceiling, I certainly pique their interest! Over the years, I have had several individuals join my team from other financial institutions. Please understand this isn't about building my team so that I can brag on my accolades. My goal is to help others see potential outside of their current employment, and, if it's the right fit, they can become wealth management advisors and work with me. In this way, I am adding value to their lives.

Forward Thinking

When I meet a new client, one of the first things I want to help them to decide is what age they would like to retire at. Some people say, "As early as possible," so we take a realist look at that. Other clients love what they do and don't plan on retiring from their place of employment until they are forced to. Still other clients are entrepreneurs, and they haven't given retirement any thought. Some clients have children or adult children; others don't have either. These factors and so many others need to be taken into account when planning for retirement, all of which require "forward thinking."

And once a client is actually retired, the question becomes, "How does one maintain a retirement plan that allows for them to live comfortably, without spending their investments too early, or without leaving more than necessary after passing away?" For these reasons, and many others, I always review my client's plan at least once a year to make sure we are on track or to take into account any changes in life and/or financial goals. As well, I am constantly analyzing market conditions—are we in a bull or bear market, or is the market flat?—in comparison to the client's investments so that I can make recommendations accordingly.

Forward thinking also means forward planning. For example, I have a client who lost her husband to cancer at a young age. When she came to me, she was full of grief over losing her spouse and worried over how she would take care of herself and her children. She also didn't know anything about her husband's financial planning, and she admitted that she hated having to even look at it with him. Before her husband died, he asked me to take care of his wife financially and to make sure that she had enough money for the rest of her life. As part of his investments, he had a $500,000 critical illness insurance policy.

Forward thinking also means forward planning.

When I told the grieving widow about her husband's insightful financial planning, her countenance brightened. I assured her that using this money with the right investment strategies would mean that she and her children would always have a roof over their heads and food on the table. I helped her set up a new retirement plan that gave her a monthly amount to live on. She could then choose what type of work she wanted to do, not what she had to do to make ends meet. While money couldn't take away her grief, it surely relieved a lot of stress.

It is sad to say that many people are passing away at a younger age, but making sure my clients have the most current financial plans in place for their situations is another way I can add value to their lives.

I have another client who is forty years old. He had been working at a job that paid the bills but wasn't something that he really enjoyed, and he felt he was stuck with this job until he retired at sixty-five. He often used the words "burned out" in any discussions we had. Recently, this client came into my office and said he was feeling overwhelmed. I was ready for some bad news, but instead he said, "I've inherited $500,000, what should I do?"

Over the next hour, we talked about his goals and desire for his life and what we could do with financial planning to make his "dream" life a reality. His inheritance meant that he could now choose to work at a job that he enjoyed and felt fulfilled doing. Over the course of several meetings, we set up a financial plan that allowed him to retire from his job at age fifty. He would then spend the rest of his life doing what fulfilled him the most.

As an investment advisor, I have clients of many different ages. For those who are young, I can have a lifelong impact on their finances. Building relationships first means my clients and I trust each other, and they don't feel the need to look at other financial institutions. Because I always have their best interests at heart, over the course of the next twenty to forty years, we'll be working together to accomplish their financial goals. I see this as adding value to their lives; they don't need to change advisors periodically and tell their story once again to a new person.

For my older clients, who are in their seventies, eighties, and nineties, I want to help them manage their money in ways that give them peace and comfort in the present, and once they pass away. Their illnesses and deaths are a part of my business and I take the financial responsibilities I have for these clients very seriously.

A Benevolent Outlook on Life

I have a saying that I have adopted in my life: "Don't squeeze the lemon to get out all of the juice." To my way of thinking, this means, "Don't be greedy, don't be selfish."

Throughout my career, my clients have had successful portfolios, meaning I have had the good fortune of being successful as well. But I have never had a material mindset, meaning that I have never been the type of person who "just needs one more dollar" and lives with a "Scrooge" mentality. Life is simply too short to live like that. Yes, it is great to enjoy the good things in life, and to provide for my family in comfortable ways. As well, it is great to be in a position where I can give freely of my time, money, and the things that I own.

For instance, if a friend of a friend is moving homes, I will volunteer to help. If someone I know needs to get away for a weekend,

I will offer my second home in the Laurentians. If I see a homeless person at a stop light who is looking for a handout, I will reach into my wallet. Whether it is a small act of kindness or a gift of benevolence, I want to give back whenever possible. If I can relieve someone's suffering momentarily, or make a difference in someone's life in the long term, I want to help when I can. I see this as respecting life and respecting humanity. Audrey Ann has this same mindset, and, as she grows, we are teaching our daughter to have this outlook as well.

I also don't limit my financial guidance and advice to my clients. Whether with family and friends, or meeting someone for the first time, if the subject of finances comes up and I'm asked for my input, I will always give it, and I feel very fulfilled when I have these opportunities.

Having said that, having a benevolent outlook on life isn't limited to being financially generous. Benevolence comes in all sorts of packages. For instance, I'm also sure you know people who give of their time to help out a worthy cause—and you may be one of these people.[16] My team and I plan a "giving day" every year. We choose a local charity or food bank where we can donate a full day of work. We use our cold-calling telephone skills to connect with businesses and individuals and explain what we are doing and why and then ask for a donation. All funds raised are used to purchase food to stock the charity's or food bank's shelves. We also give generously of our own money.

---

16 A friend of mine wrote a book for author Phil Callaway titled, *Making Life Rich without Any Money*. In the book, Callaway identifies six characteristics of "rich" people, characteristics that have nothing to do with money but have everything to do with true wealth in life.

Investment advisor group charity work, December, 2022.

Preparing for the Inevitable

I once heard the saying, "If you fail to plan, you plan to fail." This is particularly true in the financial world. We all know that life is in constant motion, but those who don't plan out their financial future can enter retirement wondering, "How am I going to survive?"

In the financial world, the principle is that your money should continue to grow as you get older. This is such an important mindset to have, because, as we all know, the only certainties in life are death and taxes. No matter the age of my clients, I want to help them prepare for these certainties. In the case of taxes, I want to help them limit their tax exposure. When it comes to dying, I want to help my clients do so knowing that those whom they leave behind are financially well taken care of.

I have the privilege of helping many of my older clients' spouses prepare for life after losing their loved one. The grief and despair they feel should not be compounded by financial unknowns. It is my job to help my clients financially prepare for the inevitable.

However, financial planning isn't limited to those who are looking to retire later in life. I had a forty-year-old client who had steady employment, and his "financial house" was in order. However, life was taking its toll on him, and he admitted to feeling burned out. He then called me one day to say that he had inherited a large amount of money. Retirement at sixty-five was no longer his goal; he had revised his plans to retire at forty-five so that he could enjoy life the way he wanted to. Over several discussions, we invested his inheritance money so that, barring an unforeseen complete collapse of the economy, his investments would last him the rest of his life.

Typically, my relationship with my clients lasts their entire lifetime, which means that I can add value to their lives over the long haul. It also means that I get to know each client on a personal basis, and I love adding new clients to my ever growing "financial family."

The Meaning of Money

Here is a general definition of money that applies to all uses: money is a medium or a vehicle that is used in exchange for various goods and services. However, money means many things to different people. Consider the points regarding how rich people view money:[17]

1. Rich people believe being wealthy is a right, while the average person believes being wealthy is a privilege.

2. Rich people believe starting a business is the fastest way to make money, while the average person believes starting a business is risky.

---

17   Kathleen Elkins, "8 Ways Rich People View the World Differently Than the Average Person," October 11, 2016, https://www.cnbc.com/2016/10/11/8-ways-rich-people-view-the-world-differently-than-the-average-person.html.

3. Rich people believe the wealthy are savvier, while the average person believes the wealthy are smarter.

4. Rich people believe building wealth takes a team, while the average person believes building wealth is an individual effort.

5. Rich people believe making money is simple, while the average person believes making money is complicated.

6. Rich people believe money is earned through thinking, while the average person believes money is earned through time and labour.

7. Rich people believe money is liberating, while the average person believes money is controlling.

8. Rich people believe in working for fulfillment, while the average person believes in working for money.

I have my own views on money.

To me, money brings freedom in life; it's the currency of freedom. The more you save and the less debt you accumulate, the more freedom you have to do the things you want to do—today and in the future. Certainly, you can do these things by yourself, but you will also greatly benefit by having a wealth management advisor on your side.

From a purely banking or investment point of view, money is a set of digits in your accounts that is either increasing or decreasing, and there is no real meaning attached. But if you invest a dollar and it grows to two dollars, and you take out fifty cents to spend, you have the freedom to spend that fifty cents on anything you want, knowing that your investments continue to grow. That's financial freedom!

Money also brings comfort. For instance, more money buys you a better mattress and pillow to sleep on. Money allows you to heat your house in the winter and cool it in the summer. It can also bring comfort to others when you meet a need, which makes you feel good.

Money can also buy time. When you work for money, you are giving away your time. But when your money works for you, you don't have to work as hard, and you have more time to do the things you want to.

Money also offers choice. This is pretty simple: the more money you have, the more choices you have, whether you are shopping for groceries, planning a vacation, or wanting to buy your loved one a gift. Sadly, when I look at many people's lives, I don't see the freedom of choices; I see struggle. I fully understand that not everyone is born with a silver spoon in their mouth. And countless people are born and raised in less-than-ideal circumstances. As I've gotten to know each of my clients, many have shared sad childhood stories, but these same people decided not to be chained to their circumstances and have risen above poverty, poor parenting, and a host of other issues. Others, like me, grew up in the middle class but wanted more for their lives, for their spouses, and for their children.

Knowing What I Wanted

In my case, I was sixteen when I told my parents, "I don't want to live life simply to pay bills and live paycheck to paycheck. I want to have the financial freedom to live life on my own terms."

When I first joined the finance industry, I quickly realized that the financial freedom clients wanted was in complete alignment with my life's goal. This also brought the realization that the more I helped my clients achieve their goals, the greater the reality of my own financial freedom. So, I poured my time and energy into educating myself regarding the financial industry, and all that is available—from products and services to subject matter experts. With a mindset of "doing the right thing for the client," I quickly learned how to scale my business. As the saying goes, "Time is money," and I was willing to put in the time necessary for my clients', and my own, financial freedom. Make no mistake; it doesn't matter what type of education an investment advisor has, or who they work for; there is a learning curve for everyone, and that curve takes time to learn.

However, from day one, I realized how scalable the wealth management business could be. I needed to exchange time for money, but eventually money would give me back time. While most of my colleagues saw their vocation as a job, I was building a business. This was a great edge. In the beginning, I knew that if I contacted five hundred people a day, I would gain clients. And if I shared my passion for this business with others, who then caught the same passion, I could grow a team. The math equation was simple: time + passion = eventual financial freedom. For my clients, this equation meant that I would help them invest in their financial future, and they could see the value I was adding to their lives. For potential team members, they could see a new and independent path to helping others gain their financial freedom while also finding their own freedom.

Through both clients and team members, this would produce a snowball effect in my business, creating a win-win-win. Adding financial value to everyone's lives meant that at some point my business would grow organically. I simply needed to find the right clients who would trust me with their finances and to hire trustworthy people, who wanted to be trained in doing this business the right way. For example, if I could manage three hundred portfolios, that would be great. But if I hired ten people who could manage three hundred portfolios, I would contribute to the lives of three thousand families. This is the essence of scaling. This is the essence of adding value. This is the essence of financial freedom!

Now, let's go back to your self-education. The next three chapters will give you a unique understanding on investment topics not typically covered.

TAKEAWAYS

- Money is simply a tool and one that is always in abundance, if you have the right mindset and understand how to grow the money you have.

- Money is no different from anything else in the way it creates reality; whatever we see and have in our physical world today was once only in our collective imagination.

- Adding value to my clients means researching the best investments possible for each client, based on their goals and objectives.

- An abundance of factors needs to be taken into account when planning for retirement, all of which require "forward thinking."

- Money brings freedom in life; it's the currency of freedom. The more you save and the less debt you accumulate, the more freedom you have to do the things you want to do—today and in the future.

Personal Takeaways

WHAT DID I LEARN? WHAT ARE MY FUTURE STEPS?

_____

_____

_____

_____

_____

_____

_____

_____

_____

_____

_____

_____

_____

_____

_____

_____

_____

_____

_____

_____

_____

_____

_____

_____

_____

_____

_____

CHAPTER 8

UNDERSTANDING ESG AND ESG INVESTING

The best way to predict the future is to create it.

—PETER DRUCKER

A s young people become a greater percentage of investors, ESG is becoming the standard by which millennials and Gen Z individuals determine where to invest. ESG incorporates *environmental*, *social*, and *governance* practices. In a 2018 survey, Bank of America and Merrill Lynch noted they could "conservatively estimate" US$20 trillion of assets growth in US-domiciled ESG funds alone over the next two decades.[18] With regulators around the world—including the Canadian Securities Administrators, US Securities and Exchange Commission, and European Commission—developing or have already introduced mandatory ESG reporting requirements, ESG is now at the forefront of the investment world.

---

18   Bank of America Merrill Lynch, "ESG Matters – US. 10 Reasons You Should Care about ESG," https://moneyinvestexpert.com/downloads/esg_matters.pdf.

While ESG metrics are not yet mandatory for companies in their financial reports, businesses are increasingly making ESG disclosures in their annual reports or in stand-alone sustainability reports. As well, institutions such as the Sustainability Accounting Standards Board (SASB), the Global Reporting Initiative (GRI), and the Task Force on Climate-Related Financial Disclosures (TCFD) are working to create standards to incorporate ESG into the investment process.

As Canadians, we can take pride in knowing that Canada is highly ranked among the top twenty oil-producing nations in the world. We can also be proud of the fact that Canada ranks second in governance and social progress and then fourth in the environment.[19]

When working with my clients, ESG investing has also become an important topic. So, I have written this chapter to give individuals an overview of what ESG means and what ESG investing entails.

A Brief History

ESG refers to the integration of environmental, social, and corporate governance factors as driving forces for investors when deciding what to invest in and for companies when making business decisions. What began as an investment strategy—because of individuals becoming increasingly concerned about environmental sustainability, respect for individuals specifically and the planet as a whole, and diversity and inclusion in the workplace—has grown to become a major platform in government policies and business strategies. One of the main philosophies for ESG investors is the desire to invest in businesses committed to accountability and sustainability and being the best possible places for employees to work.

---

19   "State of ESG in Canada," https://www.esgenterprise.com/esg-news/
       state-esg-canada-in-companies/.

In the investment world, ESG investing is also called Impact Investing, Sustainable Investing, Responsible Investing, or Socially Responsible Investing (SRI). SRI has been around for hundreds of years. For example, in the eighteenth century, leaders of the Quakers and Methodists created clear guidelines for their constituents to follow when determining which companies to invest in. Fast-forward to the 1960s, and we see that SRI became more mainstream, with investors excluding stocks and even entire industries from their portfolios based on investments in products like tobacco production or political support such as opposition to the civil rights movement.

In 2004, the United Nations created a report titled "Who Cares Wins" (WCW), which is widely considered the first main-stream mention of ESG in our modern world.[20] The report set a precedent: ESG would be required as part of financial evaluations for all companies going forward. With the United Nations (UN) focused on developing sustainable investments, at the time of the WCW report, "63 investment companies composed of asset owners, asset managers and service providers signed with $6.5 trillion in assets under management (AUM) incorporating ESG issues. As of June 2019, there [were] 2450 signatories representing over $80 trillion in AUM."[21] And in the twenty-first century, according to a *Bloomberg Intelligence* report, "Global ESG assets may surpass $41 trillion by 2022 and $50 trillion by 2025, one-third of the projected total assets under management globally, according to a new report by *Bloomberg*

---

20 "Who Cares Wins," United Nations Environment Programme Finance Initiative, 2004, https://www.unepfi.org/fileadmin/events/2004/stocks/who_cares_wins_global_compact_2004.pdf.

21 Betsy Atkins, "Demystifying ESG: Its History & Current Status," June 8, 2020, https://www.forbes.com/sites/betsyatkins/2020/06/08/demystifying-esgits-history--current-status/?sh=77b8325a2cdd.

Intelligence (BI). This trend continues the rise of ESG assets after they surpassed $35 trillion in 2020."[22]

Three Pillars

The three words that make up ESG—environmental, social, governance—are compared with three pillars that guide the modern worldview of investing. So, let's take a look at these to get a better understanding of their impact on ESG-based investing.

THE "ENVIRONMENTAL" PILLAR

This pillar focuses on how a company's actions, and its products and services, affect or impact local, national, and global environments. It is interesting to note that, according to a study by Simon-Kucher & Partners, a global consulting company, "85 percent of consumers globally reported shifting purchasing habits towards sustainable products over the past five years."[23] While universal issues such as climate change, pollution, and waste are prominent considerations, there are many other issues that are important to an ESG investor, such as:

- Use of fossil fuels and/or renewable energy
- Management of water and natural resources
- Pollution levels

---

22 "ESG May Surpass $41 Trillion Assets in 2022, but Not without Challenges, Finds Bloomberg intelligence," January 24, 2022, https://www.bloomberg.com/company/press/esg-may-surpass-41-trillion-assets-in-2022-but-not-without-challenges-finds-bloomberg-intelligence/.

23 Shikha Jain and Olivier Hagenbeek, "2022 Global Sustainability Study: The Growth Potential of Environmental Change," October 23, 2022, https://www.simon-kucher.com/en-us/blog/global-sustainability-study-what-role-do-consumers-play-sustainable-future.

- Hazardous materials
- Greenhouse gas emissions
- Carbon footprint
- Packaging and waste

THE "SOCIAL" PILLAR

ESG investors are very concerned about a company's behaviour regarding social issues. They ask questions like, "How does a company's conduct affect society as a whole?" and "What are the social repercussions of a company's activities?" The social pillar can be very subjective based on the investor's personal outlook. But on an objective investment level, this pillar incorporates the level of acceptance of business practices and operations by employees, stakeholders, investors, and customers. These might include:

- Diversity, equity, and inclusion
- Products and services, environmental concerns, and liability
- Animal testing
- Physical and mental health-related issues
- Supply chain transparency
- Human rights
- Privacy and data issues

THE "GOVERNANCE" PILLAR

This pillar highlights how a company operates internally or what is known as "corporate behaviour." Governance takes a critical look at a company's ethical actions in its business operations and the trustworthiness of a company as a whole. The ESG investor will want to know about things such as:

- Executive board structure, diversity, and compensation
- Wages, bonuses, and raises for employees
- Tax strategy and accounting practices
- Bribery, fraud, and corruption policies
- Company ethics and values
- Shareholder rights
- Transparency in policy

Having a solid understanding of these three pillars allows investment management firms and individuals to demand more transparency, fuller disclosures, and social responsibility from companies. With the massive current and future growth of ESG investments, the ripple effect is a sure sign that investing is shifting "business as usual."

ESG Ratings and Scores

For the ESG-conscious investor, the above information can quickly lead to one question: How do you know what investments are truly founded on ESG?

The answer to that question is not an easy one. Consider the following concerns noted by Canada Action:[24]

1. Individual agencies' ESG ratings can vary dramatically.

    An individual company can carry vastly divergent ratings from different agencies simultaneously because of differences in methodology, subjective interpretation, or agenda.

    Inherent biases also exist: from market cap size, to location, to industry or sector—all rooted in a lack of uniform disclosure.

---

24 "Canada's Environmental, Social, Governance (ESG) Leadership," https://www.canadaaction.ca/esg.

2. There are no standardized rules for environmental and social disclosures, nor is there a disclosure auditing process to verify reported data. Instead, agencies must apply assumptions, only adding to the subjective nature of ESG ratings.

3. Analyzing ESG factors involves a fair degree of subjectivity.

    It's possible to measure a company's carbon footprint but much harder to assess its social impact or business ethics.

    It's also hard to bundle such different and complex issues together or work out which is the most important.

4. There is a risk that ESG scores are manipulated or diluted.

    It doesn't help that there is no obligation on companies to provide intelligible or standardized reports—though lobby groups are encouraging better disclosure.

5. Private or state-owned companies are often excluded from ratings and do not disclose critical nonfinancial data, yet these companies play a vital role in the global market.

    The absence of these companies from rating agencies' measurement of ESG performance serves to distort the marketplace and its corresponding impact on investors.

6. Companies without a policy for a given ESG criteria may receive a score of zero, regardless of whether it is relevant.

    For example, some Canadian Energy companies operating solely in Alberta and Saskatchewan were given scores of 0 for their Offshore Safety Policies, among others, resulting in lower (and misleading) overall ESG ratings.

A good example of a creditable ESG rating system has been developed by Morningstar and its subsidiary, Morningstar Canada, a leading provider of independent investment research and data. Morningstar states, "Our Approach to Calculating ESG Risk. The ESG Risk

Ratings measure a company's exposure to industry-specific material ESG risks and how well a company is managing those risks."[25]

Morningstar ratings look at two main criteria: exposure and management.

EXPOSURE

"Exposure refers to the extent to which a company is exposed to different material ESG issues. Our exposure score takes into consideration subindustry and company-specific factors such as its business model."[26]

MANAGEMENT

"Management refers to how well a company is managing its relevant ESG issues. Our management score assesses the robustness of a company's ESG programs, practices and policies."[27]

As an example, based on the above criteria, the Royal Bank of Canada's ESG exposure is "medium" and its management of ESG material risk is "strong."[28]

What does this information tell the investor? While ESG is a sustainable and growing trend in the investment world, there are many issues that need to be addressed so that ESG standards and scoring are objective, credible, reliable, and consistent for all companies. With ESG having a profound effect across national and global economies— and becoming a preeminent force for national and international companies in transitioning to environmental, social, and governance

---

25   "Royal Bank of Canada," https://www.sustainalytics.com/esg-rating/royal-bank-of-canada/1007988055.

26   Ibid.

27   Ibid.

28   Ibid.

accountability—all investors must realize that ESG-based investing is a permanent and integral part of the investment world.

TAKEAWAYS

- With regulators around the world—including the Canadian Securities Administrators, US Securities and Exchange Commission, and European Commission—developing or having already introduced mandatory ESG reporting requirements, ESG is now at the forefront of the investment world.

- One of the main philosophies for ESG investors is the desire to invest in businesses committed to accountability and sustainability and being the best possible places for employees to work.

- The three words that make up ESG—environmental, social, governance—are compared with three pillars that guide the modern worldview of investing. Having the right type of insurance policy, or policies, in place is critical for your life and for your beneficiaries.

Personal Takeaways

WHAT DID I LEARN? WHAT ARE MY FUTURE STEPS?

CHAPTER 9
RECOGNIZING INVESTMENT BIAS

By the time any view becomes a majority view, it is no longer the best view: somebody will already have advanced beyond the point which the majority have reached.

—FRIEDRICH HAYEK

As humans, we have built in and learned bias. A "bias" is an unfounded or illogical inclination that we hold to be true or prejudice based on who we are and how we were raised. When it comes to money, our personal bias will direct how we make investments and our investment style. Because money is personal, it reflects and affects our life and lifestyle—and our personal bias will affect how we judge an investment. A particular bias will affect our ability to make decisions based on facts and evidence, because that bias will create an inclination to ignore whatever doesn't line up with our mindset.

Whenever an investor takes a "biased action," they are failing to recognize anything that might contradict their belief. Instead, the investor believes that the investment strategy they use will automatically lead to improved returns and greater wealth. Investment bias is affected by factors such as panic, overconfidence, and a desire for control, any or all of which can lead to poor decision-making. Therefore, it is very important to understand the different types of investment bias so that we can understand why and how we make investment choices. Here are the most common types of investment bias and how they affect our decision-making process.

Anchoring Bias

Anchoring Bias
RELYING TOO HEAVILY ON INFORMATION RECEIVED FIRST

WHAT IS ANCHORING?
Anchoring is most commonly used in facets of retail shopping, such as groceries, clothing and car shopping.

No one buying

Everyone dying to buy

$199

$500 ← Anchor

60% discount

$199

Anchoring bias is mental bias in which people tend to place a greater importance on the first piece of information they receive, regardless of the accuracy of the information. It occurs when people rely too much on preexisting information or the first information they are presented with.

For example, while considering a particular stock, an investor will check the fifty-two-week high or low price. The high and low are now the "anchor," which registers in the investor's mind. Additional information will affect how the investor sees the share price in relation to the fifty-two-week high or low. However, the high and low can be misleading because they are based on the past. For example, the current share price might look cheap in comparison to the fifty-two-week high but, in fact, might be overvalued because the publicly traded company may be losing clients, which will affect revenue. Another example is anchoring a decision based on what an analyst forecasts based on their "expert opinion." After all, the analyst is a professional, so what they are saying must be true!

Anchoring bias can be good, because it creates a baseline from which to make decisions based on limited information to determine choices. It can also make objective thinking difficult because of the constantly changing stream of information.

To overcome anchoring bias, the investor must take a critical look at why they are about to make a particular investment. Is it based on first impressions? Because the "expert" said it's the right thing to do? If the investor recognizes they have an anchoring bias, they can help themselves by being more deliberate before making a decision by gathering as much information as needed rather than simply following their instincts.

Confirmation Bias

Confirmation Bias
SEEKING OUT INFORMATION THAT CONFIRMS AN EXISTING BELIEF

WHAT IS CONFIRMATION BIAS?

Confirmation bias is the natural tendency to filter out information to retain only what confirms one's original belief.

Working against good behaviour every day	Searching out the answers that you want to hear rather than the right answers

"You're more inclined to make a new investment after having success on your most recent transaction."
—**Coreen T. Sol, CFA**

Confirmation bias is the tendency to seek information that supports the investor's beliefs, mindset, and/or viewpoint. There is a simple motive behind this bias: people have a need to be "right" and look for anything that proves their point of view, their actions, etc.

When considering investments, confirmation bias can cause people to maintain preconceived beliefs about their investments while disregarding information that contradicts the investor's mindset. For instance, a conservative investor may only consider information that takes a balanced approach to investing as opposed to an aggressive approach.

Confirmation bias can limit an investor to a particular stock or sector. For instance, the investor might only be focused on the automotive industry or natural resources and will disregard any unfavorable news about either of these sectors. However, having too narrow of a focus can make the investor vulnerable to market downturns, which can affect their portfolios' alignment with their long-term goals. This bias can also blind the investor from having a realistic view of the markets, which can lead to poor investment decisions.

Overcoming confirmation bias starts by being aware that it exists. We all have this type of bias in many areas of our lives, so it should not come as a surprise that it exists in the investment world. When this bias is in operation, the investor will gather information, and other views and opinions that support their particular belief. However, in order to have an objective outlook, the investor should look for alternative—not necessarily opposing—ideas that challenge their mindset. For example, making a list of pros and cons regarding a particular investment will help create an open mind. It is also important *not* to ask questions that will lead to confirmation about a particular investment but instead to play the "devil's advocate" and look for evidence that challenges a belief the investor is holding. The goal is to understand both sides of the investment in order to make sure this is the right one for the investor.

Recency Bias

Recency Bias

BASING DECISIONS ONLY ON THE MOST RECENT INFORMATION

WHAT IS RECENCY BIAS?

Recency bias is when individuals make decisions based on recent results, or on their perspective of recent results, which may lend itself to making incorrect conclusions based on the recent past.

"What we learn from history is that people don't learn from history. When investors get either too fearful or too greedy, they sometimes hide behind the notion that, 'This time it's different.' Usually, they regret it."
—Warren Buffett

The word "recency" refers to how *recently* a purchase has been made, how *often* it has been made, and how *much* money has been spent. In the investment world, recency bias gives greater importance to short-term performance versus long-term. For example, following a hot investment trend can lead to irrational investments, or selling securities during the COVID-19 crisis created losses that did not need to be incurred. Another example is a $50,000 investment has grown to $145,000 in eighteen months and then falls to $95,000 in the next three months. Recency bias will focus on the "loss" of $50,000 ($145,000–$95,000) rather than the gain of $45,000.

To avoid recency bias, consider the following:

- Understand that equity markets are cyclical. Bull and bear markets are commonplace, and markets always recover from bear markets and will pull back after an extended bull run. However, the overall trend of investment markets is always up, and a new peak in a bull market will always be higher than the last one.

- Keep long-term goals in mind. When an investor has clearly defined goals based on an investment plan, those goals should determine when and how to invest and not market conditions. It is important to stay disciplined in following an investment plan, in order for financial goals to be reached.

- Portfolio asset allocation. When the investor looks at their portfolio's overall performance, asset allocation is the most important factor. A regular review of the portfolio's assets and rebalancing when necessary (not simply because of market conditions) are key to getting the best portfolio performance according to the investor's goals.

- Have a financial advisor. Especially when the markets are in turbulent times, having objective advice and experience are key to "sticking to the plan."

Herding Bias

Herding Bias
FOLLOWING THE CROWD INSTEAD OF MAKING DECISIONS

WHAT IS HERDING BIAS?
Herding bias is the tendency to follow the actions of a larger group, whether those actions are rational or irrational. It is rooted in early human behaviour.

If you think about a herd of buffalo, when one gets spooked and runs, the rest follow. And when one buffalo stops to rest, the herd does the same. When it comes to investing, herd bias refers to the investor's inclination to do what other investors are doing. Emotion and instinct, rather than objective analysis, determine the investor's sentiment. Herd investing happens when an investor follows crowd investing that isn't necessarily part of the investor's goals for a financial plan. This leads to a collective mentality of buying or selling the stocks or assets in large numbers. Herd bias is a major cause of investment bubbles in which investors follow the sentiments of other investors, creating a "stampede" for a particular stock or in a specific sector. For instance, consider the 1995–2000 dot-com bubble, when investors pumped millions of dollars into internet-based start-up companies, looking for businesses that would turn a quick profit and establish long-term profitability.

The Morningstar Science Behavioural Sciences team notes that herd bias has four key drivers:

1. Investors are more prone to herding behaviour when making difficult decisions. According to Morningstar researchers Samantha Lamas and Steve Wendel, "In everyday life, when we're not sure about something, it's usually a good idea to follow the crowd. This is an example of our 'System 1' in action, in which our minds find ways to take a shortcut instead of solving a complex problem. So, if investors are not confident about their investing-related expertise, their minds may automatically choose to follow the crowd. And unfortunately, when it comes to finances, the crowd is usually running in the wrong direction."

2. Herding bias is especially prevalent during times of uncertainty. We really are in a period of flux and regime changes. It's hard to say what will be the impact of a long-lasting war in Ukraine on our lives and finances. Moreover, the previous thirty years (1991–2020) were generally marked by declining interest rates and benign inflation, creating a favorable environment for both stocks and bonds. But both measures are now reversing course.

3. Going against the crowd is emotionally draining and can even be physically uncomfortable. Our instincts tell us to fit in and not be left behind.

4. Not following the crowd requires us to engage the more rational side of our minds and make a more logical choice. Unfortunately, that requires attention, and, right now, an investor's attention is already juggling multiple concerns like the increase of energy and food prices and supply chain issues.[29]

Overcoming herd bias starts with taking a step back before making an investment and doing the necessary due diligence on a company's fundamentals and its future to see if it is truly a solid investment. Be wary of stocks being hotly promoted (often called "pump and dump") and internet forums full of amateur speculation. Next, always question those giving advice and research several sources. What are their qualifications? What connection do they have to the company specifically and investing as a whole?

Occasionally, what might seem like herd investing might simply be sound investing. For instance, the fundamentals of a stock could

---

29   Sara Silano, "What Is Herd Behaviour, and Why Does It Impact My Money?" June 23, 2022, https://www.morningstar.ca/ca/news/224170/what-is-herd-behaviour-and-why-does-it-impact-my-money.aspx.

be misaligned with the stock price; the stock might be oversold based on rumors instead of real-time analysis. The price will inevitably rise again, which could easily be mistaken for herding.

Finally, avoid speculation. Long-term goals that meet your financial objectives are not met by investing in the next "Google or Microsoft" that is based on public opinion.

Ambiguity Aversion Bias

Ambiguity Aversion
A TENDENCY TO AVOID THE UNKNOWN

WHAT IS AMBIGUITY AVERSION?

Ambiguity aversion is the tendency to avoid the unknown by having a preference for known risks over unknown risks.

Daniel Ellsberg paradox:
Select a ball from either bag and guess the colour.

1	**2**
50 red balls and 50 black balls	100 balls—red and black mixed
Probability of success: 50%	**Probability of success: ?**

RESULT

More people chose bag 1, where there was more certainty in the outcome (50% chance of guessing correctly).

Fewer people chose bag 2, where there was more uncertainty (ambiguity) in the outcome.

John R. Graham, Campbell R. Harvey, and Hai Huamg, "Investor Confidence, Trading Frequency, and Home Bias," Management Science 55, no. 7 (2009): iv–1266.

Ambiguity aversion bias occurs when investors want to eliminate uncertainly and tend to lean toward known outcomes over unknown ones. They want to avoid uncertainty by choosing what they are confident of.

Ambiguity happens when there is more than one possible outcome, which can cause confusion in the investor's mind. When making decisions, human tendency is to choose what is safe and familiar, even if facts and rationale show there is no reason to. Ambiguity bias comes to the forefront when the investor has to make a choice based on incomplete information. For instance, while it is common knowledge that investing in the stock market can increase individual wealth and create passive revenue, there are countless people who avoid the stock market like the plague. Why? Because of market volatility that produces worry, anxiety, and unfounded fear. They would rather go with investment options with steady, consistent, yet lower yields that are predictable.

One of the best ways to overcome ambiguity bias is through what is called "framing." In the investment world, this is done by putting a decision to be made inside a "frame" of questions such as: Is there really such a thing as zero-uncertainty investments? Is risk something to be avoided at all costs? When the investor questions their own mindset, they open themselves to other investment opportunities and better align with their financial plan. Once again, emotions play a big part of ambiguity bias. Emotions are based on beliefs and assumptions that can limit investment opportunities. "Framing" challenges the investor's mindset and can bring about a better sense of reality.

Myopic-Loss-Aversion Bias

Myopic Loss Aversion
EXPERIENCING MORE SENSITIVITY TO LOSSES THAN GAINS

WHAT IS MYOPIC LOSS AVERSION?
Myopic loss aversion is the combination of a greater sensitivity to losses than to gains and a tendency to evaluate outcomes frequently.

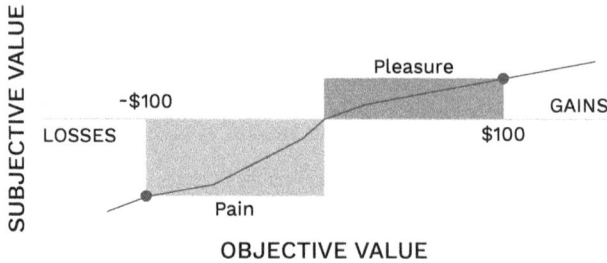

Losing $100 hurts twice as much as the feeling you'd experience by gaining $100.

Studies showed that people chose to take a risk **only when the potential gain is 2x greater than the expected loss.**

Daniel Kahneman and Amos Tversky, "Advances in Prospect Theory: Cumulative Representation of Uncertainty," Journal of Risk and Uncertainty 5, no. 4 (October 1992): 297–323, https://doi.org/10.1007/BF00122574.

Example based on experiment by Kahneman and Tversky, 1992.

The word "myopic" means "nearsighted." Myopic loss aversion is "the combination of a greater sensitivity to losses than to gains and a tendency to evaluate outcomes frequently."[30] In the investment world, this bias centers on the idea that the more an investor evaluates their

---

30 Richard H. Thaler, Amos Tversky, Daniel Kahneman, and Alan Schwartz, "The Effect of Myopia and Loss Aversion on Risk Taking: An Experimental Test," *The Quarterly Journal of Economics* 112, no. 2 (1997): 647–661, https://www.jstor.org/stable/2951249.

portfolio in the short term, the greater the chances of seeing a loss and the more loss averse the investor becomes.

For example, Peter Lazaroff, chief investment officer at Plancorp, notes, "Using historical returns on the S&P 500, you have a 47 percent chance that the market will be down on any given day. However, if you were to wait longer and look at monthly returns, that percentage drops to 38 percent. If you only look once a year at the past 12 months of returns, the chance you will see a loss drops to 21 percent."[31]

The key to overcoming myopic-loss-aversion bias is to maintain a long-term approach to investing. This means seeing volatility—market pullbacks, corrections, and bear markets—as an opportunity to buy investments at a discount. This takes mental effort and self-awareness that come about, once again, by keeping financial goals in mind based on an established financial plan. Seeing short-term volatility in light of historical charts and positive, long-term returns will prepare the investor for the unexpected, which can reduce the likelihood of making poor investment decisions during times of market downturns.

In closing, the following charts show a summary solution for each of the aforementioned biases:

---

31 Peter Lazaroff, "Myopic Loss Aversion," May 1, 2017, https://peterlazaroff.com/myopic-loss-aversion/.

Dealing with Behaviours that May Hinder Success
HOW TO ADDRESS BEHAVIORAL CHALLENGES

ANCHORING BIAS
- Acknowledge the anchor when making decisions.
- Understand, address and remember the goal—not the dollars.
- Recognize that the ways choices are presented will affect the decision.

CONFIRMATION BIAS
- Admit that different situations call for different expertise.
- Seeking out confirmation of options is a surefire way to "group think".

RECENCY BIAS
- Yesterday's truth is not tomorrow's.
- No pattern continues forever.

HERDING BIAS
- Running with the crowd may prevent solitary embarrassment but won't keep you from being wrong.
- By the time everyone is heading a particular direction, it's usually time to start heading the other way.

AMBIGUITY AVERSION
- Goal-based planning is key to success.
- Outcomes should drive your actions, not fear of the unknown.

MYOPIC LOSS AVERSION
- Financial losses are often "locked in" by panic selling.
- Keep a focus on the long-term goals in order to drive success.

"Dealing with Behaviours That May Hinder Success," Chart, Manulife Securities, Behavioural Finance, 2023.

Breaking the Behaviours
FOUR STRATEGIES TO HELP INVESTORS

1 **GET TO KNOW YOURSELF.**
Become more aware of how your tendencies can influence financial decisions.

2 **AVOID PANIC SELLING.**
Stay invested during times of market volatility and uncertainty.

3 **STAY FOCUSED.**
Don't dwell on the past; focus on your long-term goals and time horizon.

4 **CONSULT WITH YOUR FINANCIAL ADVISOR REGULARLY.**
Your financial advisor can help take the emotion out of investing.

"Breaking the Behaviours," Chart, Manulife Securities, Behavioural Finance, 2023.

It is interesting to know that Wikipedia notes that there are over one hundred identified cognitive biases.[32] Each of these can have an effect on an individual investor, depending on their temperament. The six investment biases listed in this chapter are the most common, and most investors will identify with at least one of them. The question then to ask is, "What can I do to recognize which bias(es) affect my investment decision-making and what can I do to limit the effects?"

---

32 Wikipedia, The Free Encyclopedia, "List of Cognitive Biases," last modified April 14, 2023, https://en.wikipedia.org/wiki/List_of_cognitive_biases.

TAKEAWAYS

- A particular bias will affect our ability to make decisions based on facts and evidence, because that bias will create an inclination to ignore whatever doesn't line up with our mindset.

- Whenever an investor takes a "biased action," they are failing to recognize anything that might contradict their belief.

- Anchoring bias is mental bias in which people tend to place a greater importance on the first piece of information they receive, regardless of the accuracy of the information. It occurs when people rely too much on preexisting information or the first information they are presented with.

- When considering investments, confirmation bias can cause people to maintain preconceived beliefs about their investments while disregarding information that contradicts the investor's mindset.

- In the investment world, recency bias gives greater importance to short-term performance versus long-term.

- Herd bias is a major cause of investment bubbles in which investors follow the sentiments of other investors, creating a "stampede" for a particular stock or in a specific sector.

- One of the best ways to overcome ambiguity bias is through what is called "framing." In the investment world, this is done by putting a decision to be made inside a "frame" of questions.

- The key to overcoming myopic-loss-aversion bias is to maintain a long-term approach to investing. This means seeing volatility—market pullbacks, corrections, and bear markets—as an opportunity to buy investments at a discount.

Personal Takeaways

WHAT DID I LEARN? WHAT ARE MY FUTURE STEPS?

_____

_____

_____

_____

_____

_____

_____

_____

_____

_____

_____

_____

_____

_____

_____

_____

_____

_____

_____

_____

_____

_____

_____

CHAPTER 10
AN OVERVIEW OF CRYPTOCURRENCY

Bitcoin is like everything else; it's worth what
people are willing to pay for it.
—STANLEY DRUCKENMILLER

I have long held the opinion that our current monetary system
is not sustainable. My reasoning is simple: we are a debt-driven
society, and every time our economy is in trouble, we either
borrow money from other countries or we simply print more
money. Borrowing or printing money affects interest rates, which, in
turn, affects society's buying habits and investing sentiments, which
then affect our overall economy.

A debt-driven society has a spend-today-pay-tomorrow mentality.
Consider the following:

> According to budget projections made at the time of this
> writing, the government planned to incur a $52.8 billion
> budget deficit for 2022–2023, running deficits for at least
> five fiscal years afterward.

> While the annual deficit number has dropped from the
> height of the pandemic in 2020–2021 (when the deficit

was tabulated at $327.7 billion), it would be a mistake to suggest there has been a considerable improvement in federal finances.

Deficit spending can seem like a free lunch at first glance, but there are significant costs. Running deficits means the government spends money today without the immediate cost of raising taxes to pay for it. Instead of raising taxes, the government opts to finance the additional spending through borrowing. But government debt accumulation has two important implications.

First, borrowing money means governments must pay interest on the debt annually. Federal debt interest was projected to cost $26.9 billion in 2022–2023, then climb significantly in subsequent years, reaching $42.9 billion by 2026–2027. This is money unavailable for any programs such as healthcare.

Second, the debt itself must be repaid at some point by future generations of Canadians. Budget 2022 projected that net debt would surpass $1.3 trillion that year with the government planning to add more than $100 billion in further debt within the following five years. Taxes must eventually increase or future spending must decrease to pay for today's spending.[33]

At some point, the world's economies will no longer be able to sustain its debt and will go into default. When this will happen, no one knows. And no one knows what the solution will be or what our

---

33   "Future Generations of Canadians Will Pay for Today's Deficit Spending," May 18, 2022, https://www.fraserinstitute.org/blogs/future-generations-of-canadians-will-pay-for-todays-deficit-spending.

financial system will look like. However, many people in the financial world are trumpeting cryptocurrency as the new world currency format. In today's financial world, the word "cryptocurrency" has become a mainstay.

I want to say at the outset that as of this writing, *I am not a proponent of cryptocurrency* or "crypto" as it is commonly called. However, there is speculation that by the year 2030, cryptocurrencies will make up about 25 percent of national currencies, meaning countless financial transactions will use digital currencies. If this becomes a reality, then it is incumbent upon everyone to understand the history of cryptocurrency and the current role it plays in our financial world.

The History and Rise of Cryptocurrency

As with any topic, it is important to understand its beginnings, and cryptocurrency is no exception:

> The idea for cryptocurrency first emerged in 1983, when American cryptographer David Chaum published a conference paper outlining an early form of anonymous cryptographic electronic money. The concept was for a currency that could be sent untraceably and in a manner that did not require centralized entities (i.e., banks). In 1995, Chaum built on his early ideas and developed a proto-cryptocurrency called Digicash. It required user software to withdraw funds from a bank and required specific encrypted keys before said funds could be sent to a recipient.[34]

---

34 Evan Jones, "A Brief History of Cryptocurrency," September 8, 2023, https://www.cryptovantage.com/guides/a-brief-history-of-cryptocurrency/.

An article published by *Forbes* magazine notes the following:[35]

- Although Bitcoin was the first established cryptocurrency, there had been previous attempts at creating online currencies with ledgers secured by encryption. Two examples of these were B-Money and Bit Gold, which were formulated but never fully developed.[36]

- 2008—The Mysterious Mr. Nakamoto
  A paper called "Bitcoin—A Peer-to-Peer Electronic Cash System" was posted to a mailing list discussion on cryptography. It was posted by someone calling themselves Satoshi Nakamoto, whose real identity remains a mystery to this day.

- 2009—Bitcoin begins
  The Bitcoin software is made available to the public for the first time and mining—the process through which new Bitcoins are created and transactions are recorded and verified on the blockchain—begins.

- 2010—Bitcoin is valued for the first time
  As it had never been traded, only mined, it was impossible to assign a monetary value to the units of the emerging cryptocurrency. In 2010, someone decided to sell theirs for the first time—swapping ten thousand of them for two pizzas. If the buyer had hung onto those Bitcoins, at today's prices they would be worth more than $100 million.

---

35 Bernard Marr, "A Short History of Bitcoin and Crypto Currency Everyone Should Read," *Forbes*, December 6, 2017, https://www.forbes.com/sites/bernardmarr/2017/12/06/a-short-history-of-bitcoin-and-crypto-currency-everyone-should-read/.

36 Ibid.

▫ 2011—Rival cryptocurrencies emerge

As Bitcoin increases in popularity and the idea of decentralized and encrypted currencies catch on, the first alternative cryptocurrencies appear. These are sometimes known as altcoin and generally try to improve on the original Bitcoin design by offering greater speed, anonymity or some other advantage. Among the first to emerge were Namecoin and Litecoin.[37]

As of 2022, there were almost twenty-one thousand different coins in existence, and more are sure to be added in the years to come. "A cryptocurrency is a digital currency, which is an alternative form of payment created using encryption algorithms.[38] The use of encryption technologies means that cryptocurrencies function both as a currency and as a virtual accounting system."[39] This tells us that cryptocurrency contains its own checks and balances. A cryptocurrency is a coded string of data that represents a particular currency unit. Cryptocurrency operates in similar ways to real-world currencies without having a "physical embodiment," such as coins or paper.

---

37   Ibid.

38   Encryption is a way for data—messages or files—to be made unreadable, ensuring that only an authorized person can access that data. Encryption uses complex algorithms to scramble data and decrypts the same data using a key provided by the message sender. Encryption ensures that information stays private and confidential, whether it's being stored or in transit. Any unauthorized access to the data will only see a chaotic array of bytes. Source: https://www.arcserve.com/blog/5-common-encryption-algorithms-and-unbreakables-future.

39   "The Basics about Cryptocurrency," https://www.oswego.edu/cts/basics-about-cryptocurrency.

Modern currency includes paper currency, coins, credit cards, and money accounts such as Apple Pay, Amazon Pay, and PayPal. All currencies are controlled by banks and governments, meaning that there is a centralized regulatory authority that limits how paper currency, credit cards, and financial transactions are used. However, cryptocurrency is *decentralized*. It is digital currency that operates through a computer network without any central governmental authority to validate, uphold, and maintain it. This means there are no rules regarding setting up a cryptocurrency exchange, which is where transactions take place. While there are reputable exchanges that run on powerful servers and security features, technically anyone can create their own online exchange. As of 2022, there are approximately 504 cryptocurrency exchanges that are tracked on CoinMarketCap. Exchanges use peer-to-peer networks, called "blockchains,"[40] to monitor and organize all transactions, such as buying, selling, and transferring, and also to serve as secure "ledgers"[41] of these same transactions. By utilizing encryption technology, cryptocurrencies can serve as both a currency and an accounting system.

How Cryptocurrencies Work

Cryptocurrency, also called digital currency, is a virtual method of payment that utilizes encryption to secure transactions. A cryptocurrency wallet is required to use cryptocurrencies. Blockchain networks,

---

40   A blockchain is a distributed database or ledger that is shared among the nodes of a computer network. As a database, a blockchain stores information electronically in digital format. Source: https://www.investopedia.com/terms/b/blockchain.asp.

41   A crypto public ledger is a record-keeping system. The ledger maintains the identities of participants anonymously, their cryptocurrency balances, and a record of all the transactions executed between network participants. Source: https://broker-chooser.com/education/crypto/what-is-cryptocurrency/what-is-a-crypto-ledger.

which accommodate data storage across multiple computers, are used to power cryptocurrencies. These computers are called "nodes" that validate and store the data.

There are several components needed to make cryptocurrencies a viable means of financial transactions. These components include a cryptocurrency wallet, public and private keys, and blockchain technology.

CRYPTOCURRENCY WALLET

To use cryptocurrencies, you need a cryptocurrency wallet. These wallets can be software that is a cloud-based service or is stored on your computer or on your mobile device. The wallets are the medium through which you store your encryption keys that confirm your identity and link to your cryptocurrency. It's important to understand that a wallet doesn't hold any actual cryptocurrency. It is used to hold the public and private key information needed to carry out transactions.

PUBLIC AND PRIVATE KEYS

- Public keys are similar to your bank account number. A public key is a long string of random numbers that can be shared with a third party, such as a cryptocurrency exchange, without compromising the security of your wallet. This key allows you to receive cryptocurrency in transactions—oftentimes by using a wallet address, which is essentially a compressed version of the wallet's public key.[42]
- Private keys, on the other hand, should always be kept private. A private key allows you to access the actual cryptocurrency

---

42   "What Is a Crypto Wallet?" November 4, 2021, https://n26.com/en-eu/blog/what-is-a-crypto-wallet.

on the blockchain. So, if someone has access to your private keys, it's as good as having access to the crypto in your wallet.[43]

Crypto wallets are used to keep private keys safe and accessible, allowing the user to send and receive different types of cryptocurrencies. There are several popular types of wallets currently available:[44]

- Hardware wallet: A physical device that records the private key. It could be as simple as a piece of paper or metal with the key recorded on it (these are also called paper wallets and metal wallets). There are also hardware wallets that can store crypto and connect to your other devices via USB, Bluetooth, or an app.
- Software wallet: Software wallets are browser extensions or desktop, mobile, or web apps. They may have different designs and functions, and you may have to use specific software wallets depending on the crypto you want to trade.
- Custodial wallet: Crypto exchanges control these wallets and allow users to conveniently store crypto on them. You'll create and log in to an account to use your crypto but won't necessarily have access to the private keys.
- Hot and cold wallets: Crypto wallets are described as hot wallets when they're connected to the internet and cold wallets when they're not.

To receive cryptocurrencies requires an address known as a public key. This address is found in the "generate address" feature in a wallet. The alphanumeric address or QR code is then copied and shared

---

43   Ibid.

44   Louis DeNicola, "What Are the Safest Ways to Store Crypto?" June 4, 2022, https://www.experian.com/blogs/ask-experian/what-are-safest-ways-to-store-cryptocurrency/#:~:text=In%20order%20to%20store%20your,for%20one%20over%20the%20other.

with whomever the cryptocurrency is being sent to. To send funds to another wallet requires having the address of the receiving wallet. To find this address, there is a "send" feature in each wallet in which the address of the wallet receiving the cryptocurrency is entered. Next, the amount of cryptocurrency to be sent is entered then the "confirm" button is clicked. It is always best to send a small test transaction before sending large amounts of crypto. Also, sending any type of cryptocurrency requires a fee that will be paid to miners[45] in exchange for processing the transaction.

BLOCKCHAIN TECHNOLOGY

Cryptocurrencies are powered by a technology called the *block-chain*. The word "block" means the transaction information, and the word "chain" is the linking together of that information. Therefore, a blockchain contains a record of every sent-and-received transaction specific to a particular cryptocurrency. "Each block contains a set of transactions that have been independently verified by each member of the network. Every new block generated must be verified by each node before being confirmed, making it almost impossible to forge transaction histories."[46]

Blockchains are similar to the balance sheet of a bank, making transactions possible without the need for a bank or credit card. Just like a bank's ledger contains every single transaction pertinent to the bank, blockchain tracks all cryptocurrency transactions through the

---

45 Blockchain miners are individuals who have the computer hardware and appropriate software needed to mine digital currencies or solve complex mathematical problems. The mining process is referred to as "proof-of-work," which is one way of securing the blockchain. This mechanism involves solving a mathematical problem that requires computing power provided by computer hardware. Source: https://blufol. io/who-are-blockchain-miners/.

46 Investopedia Team, "Cryptocurrency," November 3, 2023, https://www.investopedia. com/terms/c/cryptocurrency.asp.

particular network. The contents of the online ledger must be agreed upon by the entire network of an individual node or computer maintaining a copy of the ledger.

There are two basic types of blockchains: (1) open-source or public blockchains that allow anyone to use or build on a particular technology, thereby eliminating the need for a third party to verify and enable transactions, and (2) private blockchains used by corporations and other conglomerates that limit participation through the use of permissions.

There are also two types of networks that blockchains operate on:[47]

- Centralized networks are built around a single, centralized server/master node, which handles all major data processing and stores data and user information that other users can access.
- A decentralized network distributes information-processing workloads across multiple devices instead of relying on a single central server.

How Do You Buy Cryptocurrencies?

All cryptocurrencies are bought, sold, or traded on cryptocurrency exchanges or through a broker. Just like with a bank account, an account is set up and the user must be verified. Once the account is active, a cash deposit is made before placing an order for a particular cryptocurrency. Once a storage method must be chosen by the user, the cryptocurrency is kept in this location and is available 24/7.

---

47   Cryptopedia Staff, "Centralized, Decentralized, & Distributed Networks," July 12, 2021, https://www.gemini.com/cryptopedia/ blockchain-network-decentralized-distributed-centralized.

What Can You Buy with Cryptocurrencies?

In a world that is increasingly going digital, the list of items and places to shop that accept cryptocurrency is growing daily. For instance, you can purchase cars such as Elon Musk's Tesla; tech products from Newegg, AT&T, and Microsoft; Overstock, Shopify, and Rakuten are all proponents; and online money exchange PayPal allows users to buy, sell, and hold cryptocurrency in their accounts.[48]

Scams and Investment Losses

As I noted at the beginning of this chapter, I am not a proponent of cryptocurrency. I liken it to the new "Wild West" of the investment world. There is no regulation, there are few rules, and many crypto platforms are vulnerable to cyberattacks, all of which make this a buyer beware sector.

For example, in February 2022, cryptocurrency exchange platform Wormhole lost $320 million after a cyberattack.[49] In addition to this attack, cryptocurrency scammers have stolen more than $1 billion since 2021, according to a report by the Federal Trade Commission.[50]

The website Privacy Affairs highlighted the following cryptocurrency losses in 2022:[51]

---

48 Rakesh Sharma, "What Can You Buy with Bitcoin?" April 1, 2024, https://www.investopedia.com/what-can-you-buy-with-bitcoin-5179592.

49 Amanda Hetler, "11 Common Cryptocurrency Scams in 2024," January 10, 2024, https://www.techtarget.com/whatis/feature/Common-cryptocurrency-scams.

50 Ibid.

51 "Cryptocurrency Scams Statistics 2023," Privacy Affairs, accessed April 15, 2024, https://www.privacyaffairs.com/cryptocurrency-scams-2022/.

- According to Solidus Labs, threat actors in the crypto industry launch up to fifteen crypto scams per hour.
- From January to November 2022, hackers stole $4.3 billion worth of cryptocurrency. This accounts for a 37 percent increase from 2021 during the same period.
- Potentially, the largest cryptocurrency scam to date could be the collapse of FTX, where according to experts, between $1 and $2 *billion* of clients' funds continue to be unaccounted for.
- In Q1 2022, 97 percent of all stolen cryptocurrency came from DeFi protocols.
- According to the FTC, consumers lost over $1 billion from the beginning of January 2021 through March 2022 to cryptocurrency scams.
- Americans lost $329 million to cryptocurrency scams in Q1 2022.
- Australians have lost AUD242.5 million ($166 million) to investment and cryptocurrency-related scams in 2022.
- Investors in Hong Kong have lost $50 million to cryptocurrency scams in 2022.
- Scammers prefer Bitcoin (70 percent), Tether (10 percent), and Ether (9 percent) for scams.
- Social media platforms, such as Instagram (32 percent), Facebook (26 percent), WhatsApp (9 percent), and Telegram (7 percent) are used for crypto scams.
- Since 2021, most reported crypto scams and losses began with a message, a post, or an ad on a social media platform.
- Statistics show that young people (ages twenty to forty) are more susceptible to crypto scams.[52]

---

52 Ibid.

Ways to Invest

In Canada, cryptocurrency is commonly purchased on coin exchanges such as Coincase, Coinberry, Newton, Coinsmart, and Netcoins. The drawback with investing through an exchange is that every sale is taxable, meaning capital gains or losses must be reported. Until the Government of Canada decides differently, there is currently no way to directly hold cryptocurrency in a tax-advantaged account, such as a TFSA (tax-free savings account) or RRSP.

However, cryptocurrency such as Bitcoin can be purchased using an ETF. ETFs are bought and sold on all stock markets during normal trading hours, and they can be held in a TSFA account or an RRSP. The Prosper Investments Bitcoin ETF, BTCC.TO, is the first cryptocurrency ETF to be approved in Canada and trades on the Toronto Stock Exchange. The fund charges a 1 percent management fee and is invested solely in Bitcoin. Two other options are CI Galaxy Bitcoin ETF (TSX: BTCX.B) and Purpose Bitcoin ETF (TSX: BTCC.B). Keep in mind that Bitcoin, like all cryptocurrencies, is highly volatile, and investing in these ETFs should only be done by experienced and risk-tolerant investors. As well, unlike cryptocurrencies, ETFs do not trade 24/7, meaning that after-hours and weekend volatility can give the investor sudden gains or quick losses at the market's opening bell. As well, ETFs are not "currency hedged," meaning that they are subject to fluctuations between the Canadian and US dollar.

Here is something else to keep in mind. While investors are not taxed for owning crypto, there are taxable events such as:

- Selling or gifting cryptocurrency
- Trading or exchanging the cryptocurrency for another cryptocurrency
- Converting cryptocurrency into fiat

- Using cryptocurrency to buy goods

The investor must always keep in mind that every time they buy, sell, or trade cryptocurrency, it's a taxable event and needs to be reported on year-end taxes, so detailed records must be kept.

In closing this chapter, I want to reiterate that while the cryptocurrency world is ever-changing and this medium of financial exchange is becoming more acceptable, the future of digital currency is unclear and extremely volatile. Investing in any form of cryptocurrency is 100 percent risk, in my opinion. Before making any type of purchase, ask yourself this question: Can I afford to lose the money I invest in cryptocurrency without affecting my current and financial situation and my future retirement?

As you continue reading, the next chapter will give you further insights into my investment philosophy when helping my clients make the best decisions for their financial future.

TAKEAWAYS

- There is speculation that by the year 2030, cryptocurrencies will make up about 25 percent of national currencies, meaning countless financial transactions will use digital currencies.

- A cryptocurrency is a digital currency, which is an alternative form of payment created using encryption algorithms. The use of encryption technologies means that cryptocurrencies function both as a currency and as a virtual accounting system.

- There are several components needed to make cryptocurrencies a viable means of financial transactions. These components include a cryptocurrency wallet, public and private keys, and blockchain technology.

- In the world of cryptocurrency, there is no regulation, there are few rules, and many crypto platforms are vulnerable to cyberattacks, all of which make this a buyer beware sector.

- Cryptocurrency such as Bitcoin can be purchased using an ETF. ETFs are bought and sold on all stock markets during normal trading hours, and they can be held in a TSFA account or an RRSP.

- The cryptocurrency sector is for experienced investors, one that is truly speculative.

Personal Takeaways

WHAT DID I LEARN? WHAT ARE MY FUTURE STEPS?

_____

_____

_____

_____

_____

_____

_____

_____

_____

_____

_____

_____

_____

_____

_____

_____

_____

_____

_____

_____

_____

_____

_____

_____

_____

_____

CHAPTER 11

MY OWN RECIPE

If your goal is to become financially secure, you'll likely attain it, but if your motive is to make money to spend money on a good life, you're never gonna make it.
—THOMAS J. STANLEY

In case you didn't realize by now, I love my job! I enjoy working with my clients. I'm fully invested in understanding the stock market and investment vehicles, historically, presently, and in the future. I'm a "people" person at heart and always have been.

Having said that, I want to be clear that my job is focused on doing the hard work of investing.

To some, that might sound a little confusing. I don't do the hard work, the physical labour, any more than someone in the construction trades might do. But every day is a financial grind, one that I happily take on, on behalf of my clients. Typically, I'm up at six o'clock in the morning, checking the markets, doing research, setting up client meetings, setting up team meetings, scheduling seminars to attend, and much more. I also have legal and management paperwork to stay on top of, and I don't want anything to "fall through the cracks." My day usually ends around seven o'clock in the evening, but it can be later if a client wants to meet with me.

I can also state unequivocally that it is hard work building the right team under me, but I wouldn't have it any other way. Over the years, I've interviewed a number of people who have pie-in-the-sky thinking. Their mentality is that being an investment advisor is a nine-to-five job, starting right at nine and ending right at five, with paid lunches, a paid-for office, and a comfortable chair. And it's easy to look at some charts and do a little research to come up with investments that will outperform the markets in any condition—or so these people think. However, the truth is just the opposite. No one can time the markets. No one is immune to negative percentage portfolios. And investment advisors who have a get-rich-quick mentality quickly fizzle out of this business when the markets pull back or go into a recession.

What's more, when the markets head into negative territory, it is my job to calm my clients and to review their portfolios with them and to remind each person what we are doing and why we are doing it. As well, I have a team to take care of, to make sure they are doing the same thing I am with their clients. The truth is that there's a lot of negative sentiment in this business. Negativity can come from the markets all the way through to being rejected when making initial phone calls. A successful advisor needs to have "thick skin," a calm demeanor, and a future-thinking mindset.

I've been fortunate enough to be even-tempered since childhood. I rarely argue with anyone, believing that getting along is better than being at odds with someone. As well, I've always had what people call an "old soul." Certainly, I had fun with other kids my age, but I preferred to spend time with adults and figure out how I best fit into an adult world. My grandparents always told me that I was growing up too fast. I was way too serious for my age and put a lot of pressure on myself to grow up fast. At times I felt like I wanted to bypass childhood and being a teenager, go straight to adulthood. As well, I wasn't good at playing team sports such as soccer and hockey, but I sure loved motorsports like ATVs and motorbikes. Motorsports are action oriented. I'm the one in control, which is something that appeals to my risk versus reward mindset.

In school, I knew I was smart but not book smart. I received average grades because my focus wasn't on academic subjects; I simply had no interest. I have always been someone who liked to take immediate action, and academics simply never allowed me to do that. I used to spend most classes drawing and thinking instead of listening to the teachers. You should see how many different cars and race tracks I drew along the way!

The Human Connection

Another part of my personal recipe is my ability to connect with people. I call that my "human connection." I've had this ability since childhood. I am very comfortable being myself, but my temperament allows me to easily adapt to other people. For instance, if a client is full of energy and talks fast, I can adapt to their style. If a client is methodical and thinks things through, I can work with that person. I believe that having confidence in myself allows me to be adaptable.

In the world of wealth management advisors, adaptability is extremely important. People don't choose an advisor thinking that they will switch to someone else multiple times. They choose their advisor, thinking that they are entering into a long-term relationship. However, people can quickly spot someone who is phony and simply trying to gain their business, especially those who are like the proverbial snake oil salespeople. Client/investor personalities have to mesh. And a financial advisor must have more than just the client's finances as their focus; clients are people, not dollars. In my opinion, if an investment advisor doesn't care about the client's family and their extended life, they have no business managing that person's money.

Conversely, I try to avoid conflicts on any level. For instance, I don't try to convince a client of something they don't want to do. I work with my clients to help them establish goals that will give them the financial freedom they are seeking. An investment advisor is not like a lawyer or a doctor with whom you have occasional contact. Your investment advisor should be an integral part of your life throughout your lifetime. Why? Because your financial portfolio isn't like the roof on your house, which will remain the same for twenty-plus years. Financial markets change daily. Financial goals change as lifestyles change. In my case, the majority of my clients have been with me since I started in this business, and I plan on maintaining our relationship throughout their lifetime.

When I meet a potential client for the first time, I want to know who they are, what their current lifestyle looks like, and what their future plans entail. Together, we do an assessment of where they are at that particular time in their life. I'll then conduct an analysis to determine ways I can optimize their investments in comparison to their current portfolio. Honesty is always the best policy, and if I feel I can add value to their lives, I explain what I can offer and what I can do for them. If the client agrees, we then partner together to revise and optimize their portfolio. I say all of this to stress the importance of being a "people" person. If someone doesn't like working with people, then becoming a wealth management advisor isn't the right business for them.

The Effects of Money

In my years as a wealth management advisor, I've noticed that money has different effects on people. I've also noticed that it doesn't matter how little or how much a client has; they react to market changes according to their personal makeup.

Market volatility can quickly cause financial stress for the economy and for individuals. For example, I've known wealthy people who can become very insecure during times of market fluctuation. It doesn't matter if they have $2 million, $20 million, or $200 million invested in solid performing portfolios; having wealth doesn't guarantee a good night's sleep. When markets go through a downturn, people tend to focus on what they are losing and what the bottom line of their portfolio looks like. However, because the markets are always cyclical, a drop in the market can actually present the best buying opportunities. And part of my job is to recognize when these opportunities present themselves.

Being empathetic and a good listener is integral to my job. I fully understand why I rarely get calls from clients when the markets are heading up, but I sure get more calls when the markets head down. During these times, my position as an advisor is similar to the captain of a ship. It is my job to keep my hands on the wheel and steer my clients' portfolios through financial "rough waters," knowing that "calm waters" and "sunny skies" are ahead of us. No one can predict how long a downturn or market rally will last, but I can tell you with full certainty that both will happen.

Empathy and good listening skills help me to understand my clients' concerns, giving me the opportunity to review their portfolios with each client and, if needed, to make financial course corrections that keep the portfolio on track toward their goals and objectives.

Reviewing a client's financial goals together gives them the reassurance that their retirement plan was created to make sure they have enough wealth for the rest of their lives. Whether that plan is risk adverse or based on risk/reward, my client knows in their mind what we are doing and why we are investing in a particular way, which brings peace of mind.

In my view, this is particularly important when working with a potential client. Honesty *and* authenticity are always the best policy. If a potential client truly has a solid portfolio, I tell them so. But if I feel I can show them a better way to achieve their financial goals, I owe it to the potential client to share my thoughts and strategies. Otherwise, I won't sleep well at night!

People are resistant to change, and I understand that, especially when it comes to investments. There have been times when I've reviewed a potential client's portfolio, and it is obvious to me there are better funds, stocks, bonds, and more that could bring the client a much better rate of return. I've reviewed portfolios that, to the trained eye, simply won't meet the individual's long-term goals and objectives. When a potential client is in this position, I call it "hitting the wall." For instance, if a person plans on retiring at sixty-five, yet they are spending more than they are investing, it is my job to tell the person of the consequences they are facing. Do they want to be forced to work until they are seventy or seventy-five years old because they didn't save and invest wisely today? Has their current advisor told them this might happen?

I find it curious that, even after showing a potential client a better way to save and invest, I might still hear, "Thanks but no thanks." I also remind my team members of this reality. For these people, I wish them well, but there is a part of me that is disappointed for them as well.

How Advisors Build Their Clients' Portfolios

Here is something you may not know and is seldom talked about in professional wealth management circles. In our industry, there are two ways of growing your clientele or your "book of business."

At other companies, the first and easiest method is for a junior advisor to work under a senior advisor. The junior advisor will hopefully learn all that they can from their senior mentor, gaining knowledge, wisdom, and experience. That sounds very noble. However, consider that (1) the junior advisor is paid a salary, so their income is not correlated to the performance of their portfolios; and (2) when the senior advisor feels their junior counterpart is ready, or when the senior advisor is ready to retire, the junior advisor has the option to literally *buy* clients from their senior counterpart.

The problem I see with this business development method is that, in my view, the junior advisor never really puts in the hard work necessary to grow their clientele. I feel that handing the junior advisor everything they need on a silver platter means there is no need for the advisor to work hard on behalf of their clients in the short term in order to achieve long-term success. It's easy to take your clients for granted if they are given to you, or if you bought your way into the business versus someone who had to convince every single client to trust them with their money, which is a very different philosophy.

The second—and definitely the hardest—way a wealth management advisor builds their client list is the way my team and I do this. I'll call this the "Camille Estephan" method. Both junior and senior advisors are paid a percentage based on their AUM, which is directly related to the overall, collective performance of the portfolios. Building our AUM starts with cold-calling and convincing clients that you are the right investment advisor for them, which, in my opinion, is also the honest way. It teaches my team and me to truly value each client and to work hard on their behalf to continually earn their trust.

Camille is the founder of Diligence Wealth Management, with the first branch being established in Montreal. He built the company the old-fashioned way—one client at a time, earning their trust, and doing what is best for the client. Nobody ever paid Camille a salary; he had to earn his keep. While our administrative team members are paid a salary, advisors are paid a percentage based on the collective and overall performance of their AUM. This means that an advisor's income can be higher or lower, based on their AUM. This puts the responsibility on the advisor to always have their clients' best interests in mind.

Like Camille, every one of our advisors must build their own clientele. And this is done through the five-hundred-calls-a-day system that I talked about in chapter 4. In the early days of Diligence, this is exactly the system that Camille developed. If you think about how hard it is to gain a client through this method, you can realize how valuable each client is to their wealth management advisor. It took a lot of hard work for the advisor to gain the client's trust, so the advisor will continue to work hard for the client. The advisor knows just how much each client is worth to them—and I don't mean financially. Work and worth are tied together, and the harder an advisor works for their clients, the more the client is worth to the advisor because of the time and effort they put into the advisor-client relationship.

I call developing the client relationship the "grind" side of this business. Historically, the advisor has had to "grind" through almost two thousand no-thank-you rejections in order to connect with a couple of people who eventually become clients. Having developed my business this way, I know how valuable each client is, which makes me work hard for each person to develop a plan for their financial freedom.

BUILDING CLIENTELE

When other financial institutions hire someone new, they look at things like the school the person graduated from and what degree(s) they might have. Then, after some preliminary training, the new hire is told to find their clients by starting with family and friends. The problem is that family and friends are limited in number. And once the new hire has gone through their list of people, how do they find new clients? Most of these people are stuck because they have never learned how to connect with a complete stranger or how to develop a relationship built on trust. However, the new advisor doesn't have to worry too much; they have a salary to support them. The truth is that a family member or friend might trust the new advisor with $100,000, or $1 million. But for a total stranger to do the same is a whole new game.

In my view, an advisor cannot become truly client-centerd if they only develop clients from their "warm" market (the people they know). However, as I well know, if a client is gained after the advisor has made two thousand calls, that same

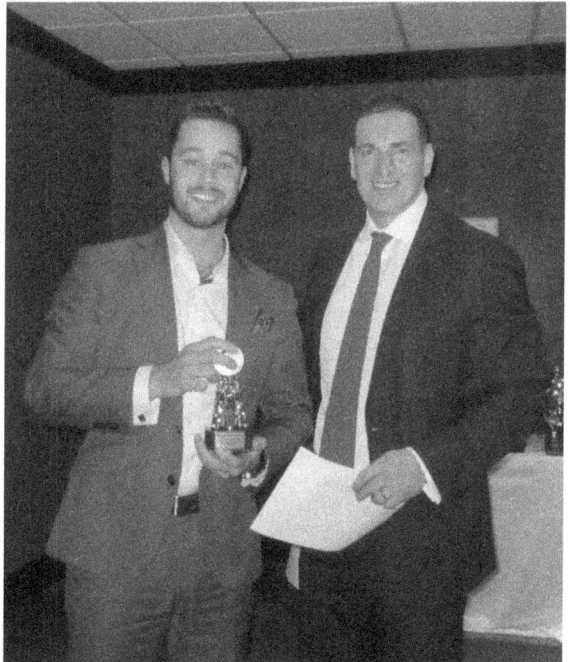

Francis and Camille, while Francis was receiving an award in 2017.

client is valued throughout their lifetime. This is the best lesson a wealth management advisor can learn. An advisor would do all they can for each client, knowing how hard they have to work to gain each client. We can all thank Camille for this methodology—because it works!

It is also very important that advisors have the latest research available at all times. I want all advisors who work within my organization to be successful, and so our branch has an investment research team. Their job is to research market conditions and the effects on various investments, that is, stocks, funds, ETFs, and so on, and to pass this information on to the advisors. This allows the advisors to focus on the relationship with their clients and give them the best advice possible.

As this chapter comes to an end, I want to reiterate the passion that a wealth management advisor must have for this business. Money is representative of each client's life—how they want to live, the goals they want to achieve, and the financial freedom they are seeking. I stress the following to my team and live by it myself: if you follow Camille Estephan's methodology, it will lead you to the right clients at the right time. Be passionate about what you are doing, and you will never lose your desire to do what is best for your clients. Maintaining a "human connection," and doing what is best for the client, is always the best path to follow. That is my personal recipe, and it is what my team and I strive to follow each and every day!

Now, let's continue with your self-education. In the next chapter, you'll gain a good understanding regarding two types of individuals that people typically turn to for investment guidance. This will allow you to choose the right person for you!

TAKEAWAYS

- No one can time the markets. No one is immune to negative percentage portfolios. And investment advisors who have a get-rich-quick mentality quickly fizzle out of this business when the markets pull back or go into a recession.

- People don't choose an advisor thinking that they will switch to someone else multiple times. They choose their advisor, thinking that they are entering into a long-term relationship.

- And a financial advisor must have more than just the client's finances as their focus; clients are people, not dollars.

- Honesty *and* authenticity are always the best policy.

- Because the markets are always cyclical, a drop in the market can actually present the best buying opportunities.

Personal Takeaways

WHAT DID I LEARN? WHAT ARE MY FUTURE STEPS?

_____

_____

_____

_____

_____

_____

_____

_____

_____

_____

_____

_____

_____

_____

_____

_____

_____

_____

_____

_____

_____

_____

_____

CHAPTER 12

DO I NEED AN INVESTMENT ADVISOR OR PLANNER?

A wise person should have money in their
head, but not in their heart.
—JONATHAN SWIFT

Throughout my years in the wealth management industry, the question I'm most often asked is, "Why do I need an investment advisor?"

To answer that question, think in terms of your home. Are you a jack-of-all-trades who can fix everything that breaks, or have you called in a professional when needed, including doing any painting or decorating? If you are not an electrician, would you wire your own basement during renovations? My point is that there are things in life that you shouldn't improve or compromise on, and your investments is one of those areas.

A proficient investment advisor will have a team of experts to help you, such as tax specialists, estate lawyers, accountants, and notaries. As well, your advisor will not be reacting to information that comes out on the six o'clock newscast, which is already old news that is too late to react to.

An advisor or planner is ready to help you develop a financial plan and strategy that will accomplish your financial goals. This individual acts as a sounding board, so you can express your thoughts rather than keep everything bottled up in your mind. The truth is that most people are not experts when it comes to finance; however, that is exactly the role an advisor or planner takes on. You want your investments to grow so that when retirement comes, you can continue to pay your utilities, go on vacations, or whatever else you have in mind. You want your investments to last you a lifetime, and your financial advisor or planner can help you set yourself up for success.

So, why do you need an advisor or planner?

The answer to this question comes by answering two other questions: "Do you have the time necessary to devote to developing and following a financial plan?" and "Do you have the experience necessary to follow a financial plan and know when and how to adjust it according to market conditions and long-term goals?" If you can answer "Yes" to these two questions, then you are to be congratulated for setting yourself up for success.

However, for the majority of people, the answer to the above two questions is "No." It leads back to the first question, "Why do I need a financial advisor?" Let's explore this together.

The Value of Advice

Let's say you have some experience in investing. You could always buy index funds and save on the fees paid to an investment advisor. However, as I've noted before, the problem with investing is that money becomes emotional during times of market volatility. Should you stay invested in the stock market? Pull out and buy bonds? How do you know when to stay in and when to divest?

Your investments represent your life, so naturally you want to protect your assets as well as invest in the right assets at the right time. But when emotions take control, individual investors tend to try to time the market, jumping in during advances and pulling out during pullbacks. The problem is that no one can time the market. When stocks pull back, emotions tell the investor to hit the sell button. However, as the following chart shows,

Francis recognized as a 5-star advisor in Canada, 2021.

trying to time the markets—investing when the markets are good and pulling out when they are dropping—can significantly lower returns for longer-term investors:

Stay Invested So You Don't Miss the Market's Best Days

$10,000 INVESTED IN THE S&P 500 (12/31/06 – 12/31/21)

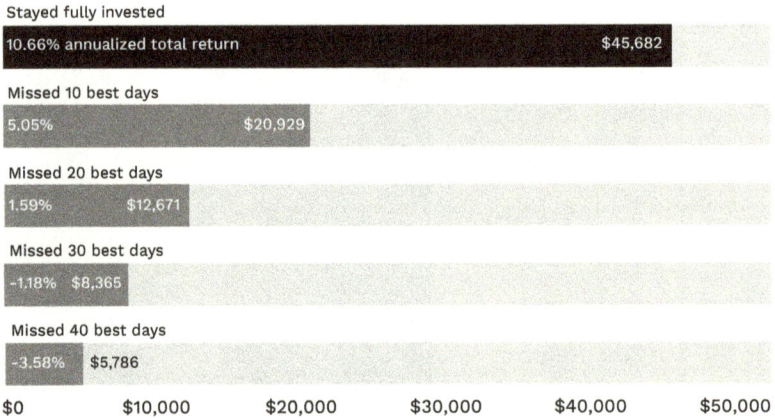

Stayed fully invested
| 10.66% annualized total return | $45,682 |

Missed 10 best days
| 5.05% | $20,929 |

Missed 20 best days
| 1.59% | $12,671 |

Missed 30 best days
| -1.18% | $8,365 |

Missed 40 best days
| -3.58% | $5,786 |

$0 $10,000 $20,000 $30,000 $40,000 $50,000

By staying fully invested over the past 15 years, you would have earned $24,753 more than someone who missed the market's 10 best days.

Pippa Stevens, "This Chart Shows Why Investors Should Never Try to Time the Stock Market," CNBC, March 24, 2021, https://www.cnbc.com/2021/03/24/this-chart-shows-why-investors-should-never-try-to-time-the-stock-market.html.

The best thing about working with an advisor or a planner is that this individual is not emotionally tied to your investments. They have an objective outlook and can offer you a constant reminder of your financial plan and goals. While you ultimately make investment decisions, it's always best to have a "second opinion."

ADVISORS AND PLANNERS ARE TRUSTED BY CANADIANS

Trust is the foundation of all relationships, and it's vitally important for Canadians to have trust in the investment advice they are given. A white paper written by the Investment Funds Institute of Canada, the voice of Canada's investment funds industry, titled "Financial Advice in Canada," issued in November 2022, shows the following:

> The Canadian Pollara Investor Survey has run for 17 years and consistently demonstrates high levels of satisfaction with financial advisors. The 2022 survey found that 92 percent of mutual fund and ETF investors are satisfied with their advisers.[53]

The same white paper states,

> Through three separate years of investigation, the researchers found that Canadians using a financial advisor accumulated substantially more assets than comparable non-advised investors. The impact of advice varied across the studies and associated economic conditions. The research found that after 15 years, investors accumulated 2.7 times more assets in 2010, 3.9 times in 2014 and 2.3 times in 2018 than comparable non-advised investors. In explaining why advised investors saved more, the researchers identified higher savings rates, a greater allocation of non-cash investments, and disciplined behaviours acquired through financial advice (for example, not selling through market downturns).[54]

Finally, the white paper notes,

> For many years, the Pollara Investor Survey has asked mutual fund and ETF investors several questions on the perceived value of advice. In 2022, 80 percent of mutual

---

53 Investment Funds Institute of Canada, "Financial Advice in Canada," November 2022, https://www.ific.ca/wp-content/themes/ific-new/util/downloads_new.php?id=27821&lang=en_CA.

54 Ibid.

fund investors and 73 percent of ETF investors state that they believe that they get a better return on investments due to their financial advisor and 84 percent of mutual fund and 78 percent of ETF investors feel more confident that they will reach their investment goals when using a financial advisor. Furthermore, 74 percent of mutual fund investors and 68 percent of ETF investors state that, because of their advisors, they have better saving and investment habits.[55]

Financial Advisor or Financial Planner?

When choosing someone to help you plan out your financial future, the first question to ask is, "Are you a financial advisor or a financial planner?" While these terms are often used interchangeably, they do not mean the same thing.

As with all experts, what separates financial planners and advisors is their level of education, training, experience, and qualifications. Whether you choose an investment advisor or a financial planner, the individuals should have at least one professional designation, such as Certified Financial Planner (CFP) or Chartered Investment Manager (CIM).

FINANCIAL ADVISORS

A financial advisor is a broad term for professionals who help manage money for individuals and institutions. This individual is paid to either help or directly manage investments, buy or sell stocks, or create comprehensive estate and tax plans. They may also hold other credentials, such as licensed insurance agent, depending on the services they

---

55   Ibid.

provide. Therefore, "financial advisor" is a broad term for someone involved with money management or financial products and services such as life insurance, real estate, or accounting services. They can also help place short-term trades or even provide banking services. For example, a financial advisor who specializes in securities is called an investment advisor.

FINANCIAL PLANNERS

Professional financial planners are individuals who help their clients develop financial strategies to meet long-term financial goals and act as personal finance mentors. There is no single private or governmental body that oversees the financial planning industry, and regulation is provided by the type of services that the planner provides.

There are three common designations: CFP, Personal Financial Planner, and RFP, and each designation comes with its own requirements. Financial planners can offer a variety of services, such as:

- creating a financial budget;
- identifying ways to save on taxes;
- assisting in retirement planning;
- offering estate planning advice;
- planning retirement;
- planning college tuition;
- assessing and recommending insurance protection; and
- consulting with estate planners, tax planners, and other advisors.

ONLY IN QUEBEC

In Quebec, only certain trained individuals are allowed to use the title "financial planner." The title is "planificateur financier" or the acronym "Plan. Fin." in French. This includes financial planners who:

- have certification that has been issued by the Autorité des marchés financiers and
- are members of a professional association with which the Autorité des marchés financiers has entered into an agreement.

THE DIFFERENCE

The goal for both financial advisors and financial planners is to provide helpful advice and guidance that align with the client's financial plan and goals. However, there are some differences to keep in mind when choosing between an advisor and a planner. For example, some financial advisors work with their clients over a long period of time, while others only help with specific transactions or investments. Financial planners, on the contrary, tend to take a more holistic approach to client finances and develop long-term plans that address all aspects of a client's financial life. These are usually revisited every few years, with client investments or strategies adjusted as plans are updated.

Another key difference is that financial advisors may earn commissions on some of the products they sell, while financial planners more commonly charge hourly or flat fees for their services.

Finally, while financial advisors and planners often have many of the same licenses, they typically have different certifications—including the CFP designation.

How Advisors/Planners Are Paid

How your advisor/planner is paid will have an effect on the overall net performance of your portfolio. As well, the size of your portfolio might determine whom you select to help you.

In Canada, there are four main ways financial advisors/planners are paid: client fees, commissions, salary, and bonuses. In most cases, advisors are compensated in a combination of these ways.

CLIENT FEES

The client pays the advisor/planner either directly (fee-only) or indirectly (fee-based) for their services. While there are no set rules, generally speaking, investors with portfolios under $1 million will incur annual fees from 1.50 to 2.5 percent. Investors with a portfolio of $1,000,000 or more will incur fees of 1–1.65 percent. And those with portfolios above $5 million will incur fees below 1.00 percent.

In Canada, there are four main ways financial advisors/planners are paid: client fees, commissions, salary, and bonuses.

COMMISSIONS

The commissions can be in the form of upfront fees and transaction commissions. As of June 2022, upfront fees on mutual funds have been banned in Canada, because there has been a lot of abuse in the past from mutual fund representatives. Transaction commissions are usually a flat fee or perhaps 1 percent of the transaction and are commonly used for stock-based investments. For example, if you bought $100,000 worth of shares of a stock, it could cost $1,000 for the transaction fee.

SALARY AND BONUS

Financial advisors/planners working as employees for a financial institution usually receive a base salary with the potential to earn additional client fees, commissions, and bonuses. Bonuses are earned when criteria specific to the institution are met.

> **A word of caution:** Most advisors/planners want to give sound advice, but some may be influenced by outside sources. For example, some who are paid by commission may try to encourage you to invest where they will earn the highest commission. Salaried professionals might be incentivized to promote their own company's products and services. This leads to the next section about the importance of asking questions.

Questions to Ask

When meeting with a financial advisor or planner for the first time, you may feel excited or a little nervous. You might feel that it's necessary to tell this person about yourself and your goals, to see if they can help. The natural answer would be, "Yes, I can help!" So, it's important to take a step back and ask this individual some questions *before* giving your information to them. Questions such as the following:

- Do you work directly for a company, or do you run your own business within the company?
- Who is your ideal client?
- Who is not your ideal client?

- How do you help your ideal client determine their goals and create a plan to achieve them?
- What common problems does your ideal client face and how do you help solve them?
- What is your payment structure and how do you get paid?

If the planner/advisor gives you clear answers and takes the time to explain their guidance and direction, and you don't get a "gut-check," then it could be a good fit. Also make sure you genuinely like this person; hopefully, you'll be working together for a long time. However, at all times the famous saying "caveat emptor"—buyer beware—must be remembered.

These questions should take about ten minutes to ask and answer. If you are comfortable in continuing the conversation, here are some additional questions:

1. What are your certifications, qualifications, and credentials?
2. Do you work with a team? If so, tell me about your team members.
3. How do I contact you and/or your team?
4. How do I access my portfolio?
5. Which bank or trust has supervision of my assets?
6. How do you interact with that institution?
7. Have you or any of your team ever been sanctioned or been penalized by a regulatory authority?

At this point, you'll want to know about the products and services the advisor/planner offers. You want to be comfortable knowing to offer a wide range including, stocks, bonds, mutual funds, interest bearing accounts, ETFs, and much more. Also, you may want to know about financial planning, budget preparation, life insurance, tax help and preparation, and so on. The point is that you don't need to limit, or you can choose to limit, how much business you do with one individual.

Next, you want to be comfortable with the advisor's/planner's investment style. While you, the investor, will determine your own comfort level from conservative to speculative risk-taking, here are some things that will be important to know:

- How often are trades made or assets bought and sold within your portfolio?
- How is asset allocation determined?
- What is the basis for revising asset allocation?
- How is the percentage of increase determined in order to meet financial goals?

Here is a sample asset allocation chart:

Capital Market Strategy Illustrative Asset Mix

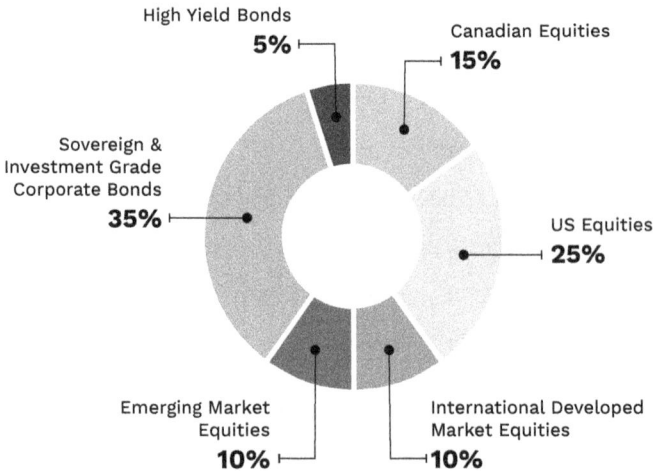

High Yield Bonds
5%

Canadian Equities
15%

Sovereign &
Investment Grade
Corporate Bonds
35%

US Equities
25%

Emerging Market
Equities
10%

International Developed
Market Equities
10%

Manulife Investment Management, Capital Markets Strategy, "Capital Market Strategy Illustrative Asset Mix," chart, data as of December 31, 2022.

Keep in mind that no one knows how assets will perform in the future. Volatility is to be expected and typically lasts for the short term. So, a portfolio built on diversified holdings with solid companies will do well over the long term. However, be wary of advisors/planners who "guarantee" a particular percentage of return or paint a you'll-always-make-money picture.

Retirement Planning

The goal of having a well-laid-out financial plan is to give you the resources to retire comfortably and when you're ready. However, with inflation continuing to take a bit out of all financial investments, running out of money in retirement is a common worry. An article published by CTV News states:

> According to a new survey, commissioned by debt specialists Bromwich+Smith and financial institution Advisorsavvy, four in 10 older Canadians say they have delayed or plan to delay their retirement because they have too much debt amid cost of living increases.

> The Survey, which was conducted between June 9 and June 12, 2022 by Angus Reid, found that 62 percent of those aged 55 or older have delayed retirement because they don't have enough savings or investments.

> The survey also found that 63 percent of older Canadians are worried about never being able to retire, while 71 percent

said they feared running out of money after they retire or having to return to work (24 percent).[56]

While these seem like dire statistics, with professional guidance and help, a financial plan can be created that lays any worries to rest, barring a complete collapse of the economy. A competent financial advisor/planner can provide direction on managing workplace pensions, how best to split pension income with a spouse, and scheduling systematic withdrawals from an RRSP, a registered retirement income fund (RRIF), or an LIRA.

A financial advisor/planner can also help you do the following:

- Determine when to convert an RRSP to an RRIF, which can be done at any age
- Determine if and when buying an annuity is the right thing to do
- Determine the best age to start collecting CPP and OAS payments
- Determine when to downsize your place of residence and/or secondary residence and how to invest or live off the profits
- Determine estate planning including minimizing tax liabilities

Artificial Intelligence versus Human Advisor

As we know, AI, artificial intelligence, is making its presence felt in every sector of our economy and every part of society at large. At

---

56 Brooklyn Neustaeter, "Recession Concerns Have Older Canadians Worried about Retirement, Pension Plans," June 17, 2022, https://www.ctvnews.ca/business/recession-concerns-have-older-canadians-worried-about-retirement-pension-plans-1.5950096#:~:text=The%20survey%20also%20found%20that,work%20(24%20per%20cent).

the time of this writing, I'm not a proponent of AI for investing if only for the simple fact that, when it comes to money, my opinion is that people need people. AI cannot get to know a person on a personal level to really understand their plans and goals. For instance, a client might say they want to maximize the money they leave to their kids but are really worried about how much inflation will cost them in terms of lifestyle and how long their money will last. AI cannot determine what is "factual" and what are human nuances. As well, AI programs are created by humans, which means there will always be a natural bias from which AI cannot protect itself against.

This isn't just my point of view. One of the world's biggest wealth managers, Ralph Hamers, the CEO of UBS—a global firm providing financial services in over fifty countries—doesn't see how AI can replace the role of financial advisors and planners. Hamers notes that AI is, "better suited to handling day-to-day functions like opening an account or executing trades than advising clients. There is no added value for client advisors to be engaged in a process like that ... They're advisors. They should advise."[57] He also notes, "that AI could be used to make sense of the research and other data that advisors don't have time for. That is what artificial intelligence can do, because even our client advisors can't read all the research that is there."[58]

The next chapter will wrap up my investment philosophy, giving you a good understanding of how I work with my clients.

---

57   Ryan Browne, "Artificial Intelligence Won't Replace the Role of Financial Advisors, UBS CEO Says," June 17, 2021, https://www.cnbc.com/2021/06/17/ai-wont-replace-financial-advisors-ubs-ceo-says.html.

58   Ibid.

TAKEAWAYS

- When emotions take control, individual investors tend to try to time the market, jumping in during advances and pulling out during pullbacks. The problem is that no one can time the market.

- As with all experts, what separates financial planners and advisors is their level of education, training, experience, and qualifications. Whether you choose a financial planner or a financial advisor, the individuals should have at least one professional designation.

- In Canada, there are four main ways financial advisors/planners are paid: client fees, commissions, salary, and bonuses. In most cases, advisors are compensated in a combination of these ways.

- It's important to take a step back and ask the advisor/planner some questions *before* giving your information to them.

- A competent financial advisor/planner can provide direction on managing workplace pensions, how best to split pension income with a spouse, and scheduling systematic withdrawals from an RRSP, RRIF or LIRA, all of which can help clients have confidence knowing their financial future is in good hands.

Personal Takeaways

WHAT DID I LEARN? WHAT ARE MY FUTURE STEPS?

CHAPTER 13

THINKING BEYOND THE CURVE

Rich people believe "I create my life." Poor
people believe "Life happens to me."
—T. HARV EKER

I love the weekends, and I'm sure you do too!

For most people, the weekends are time to catch up on life with families, doing things together, relaxing, or whatever takes them away from the nine-to-five weekday world. In my case, I spend time on the racetrack, which is my passion. But the three loves of my life are my fiancé, Audrey Ann, and my daughters, Sofia and Olivia. Audrey and I now realize what all parents know—kids demand time and attention. But Audrey and I wouldn't have it any other way; family comes first! So, I try not to answer work-related messages or reply to work-related emails, unless there is an emergency.

However, when Monday morning comes, I'm all business. Ever since entering the work world, I've had the ability to switch gears, to switch my mind from pleasurable weekends to the business week. Even today, no matter how tired I might be from sleepless nights caused by taking care of my daughters, or a weekend get-together with friends that went long into the morning hours, my mind goes into "business gear" every weekday morning. Years ago, I heard a phrase that has always stayed with me: where focus goes, energy flows. When I'm at home, my focus is on my family, so they get all of my energy. During business days, I'm focused on helping my clients create financial portfolios that help each person achieve their financial independence.

Our family at Sofia's two year birthday party.

Financial freedom allows Audrey to stay at home with Sofia and Olivia. In fact, Audrey feels that focusing her time and efforts on our daughters is her "calling." She is a brilliant businesswoman in her own right, but she has put any business endeavours on hold for the foreseeable future, and I fully appreciate her doing so.

This might sound old-school, but I have always had a "hunter" mentality. What I mean is that I love going out every day to work so that I can provide for my family. When I walk into my office at home or at the Diligence building, I know that my home front is secure and I'm fully focused on business. During the workweek, Audrey knows that I may have to work late hours or be gone from home for a couple of days. She has always been understanding, and I have always provided for our family, so this is truly a win-win for all of us. As with all relationships, Audrey and I have learned the value of compromise and what it means to "add value" to each other.

I mention all of this because I want my clients to know that when I'm focused on each one of them, I am fully focused. Because I love the financial world and all that it entails, I am committed to doing what is best for each client.

Preparing Today for Tomorrow

Here is a universal truth that no one can deny: it is impossible to predict the future. If we could predict that, we would be like Noah when he built the Ark on dry land when the sun was shining bright and there wasn't a cloud in the sky. This is just as true in the financial world. However, while we cannot predict *exactly* what will happen to the national and global economies or when it will happen, what we do know for sure it that economies, and by extension financial industries, will go up and down. Consider the following events:

- The 1929 Stock Market Crash
- The 1973 Oil Embargo
- The 1980s Recession
- 1987 Black Monday
- The 2001 Dot-Com Crash
- The 2008 Great Recession

These are six of the major downturns that have caused havoc to the US economy and, by extension, to the Canadian economy. Globally, there have been multiple crises. Here are just a few:

- Secondary banking crisis of 1973–1975 in the United Kingdom
- Latin American debt crisis (late 1970s, early 1980s) known as "lost decade"
- Japanese asset price bubble (1986–1992)
- 1998 Russian financial crisis
- 2002 Uruguay banking crisis
- 2008–2011 Icelandic financial crisis
- 2015 Chinese stock market crash
- And we cannot forget COVID-19

In each and every financial crisis, panic sets in. Individuals, companies, and financial institutions are crying out, "Sell, sell, sell!" But, to use a proverbial illustration, when Chicken Little is decrying, "The sky is falling!" everyone forgets that economies and financial markets will *rebound*. Reality tells us that recessions will happen, and nobody, not even Warren Buffett, the Wizard of Wall Street, can predict when. However, when the markets bottom out, they grow historically after every negative event, as the following chart illustrates:

What History Has Taught Us

S&P 500 INDEX: 10 WORST TRADING DAYS (%)

DATE	1-DAY DRAW-DOWN	RETURN AFTER 1 YEAR	RETURN AFTER 3 YEARS	RETURN AFTER 5 YEARS	RETURN AFTER 10 YEARS
10/15/08	-9	24	41.4	109	275.4
12/01/08	-8.9	39.3	62.9	146.3	315
09/29/08	-809	-1.5	12.2	69.9	226.4
10/09/08	-7.6	20.9	40.5	103.5	292.2
10/27/97	-6.9	23.4	62	8.7	102.5
08/31/98	-6.8	39.8	22.5	13	60.1
11/20/08	-6.7	48.8	68.7	164.3	334.5
08/08/11	-6.6	28.1	82.2	117	NA
10/13/89	-6.1	-5.8	35.6	63.8	396.3
11/19/08	-6.1	39.2	58	147.5	312.8

Manulife Investment Management, "What History Has Taught Us," Refinitiv, data as of March 2020, accessed April 15, 2024, https://www. manulifeprivatewealth.com/ca/en/viewpoints/market-update/making-sense-of-market-drawdown-what-history-has-shown-us.

My job is to help my clients build a financial "Ark" today, knowing that "bad weather" and "unpredictability" are going to happen in the markets. After COVID-19 ravaged the global economy, in North America, we also had several years of low interest rates driving inflation ever higher, and all three—COVID-19, interest rates, and inflation—created a perfect storm for a market downturn. The stock market dropped, real estate dropped, and the bond market dropped, so there were no "safe" havens.

In times like these—knowing that the markets will rise once more—it is my job to help my clients rebalance their portfolios and use instruments like nonregistered investments that can be used to capture capital losses. These can then be used against future or past capital gains to save on taxes so my clients can benefit from the situation. In fact, capital losses can be used up to three years prior to erase some past capital gains. This is a common tax strategy, one that can be used to quiet "Chicken Little." We can also sell investments that dropped slightly and add these to the blue-chip stock portfolio that my clients might hold for a very long time. There really is an opportunity in every crisis!

A Personal Financial Psychologist

Here is something I cannot stress enough: money is emotional. When markets fall, there is an underlying cause, but the fall is compounded by the negativity that surrounds the markets. The opposite is true when markets rise. There are always underlying data to support it, but the rise is compounded by the positive emotions that people feel. Even though I'm still relatively young, I've seen the emotional effect on markets play out over and over again.

While I don't have a degree in psychology, being a "voice of reason" and having a calming effect on my clients are part of my job. When a client is in a panic, wondering what will happened to their portfolio, my job is to help them refocus on the long term: What were the goals that were set up when the portfolio was initially created? Have these changed? Do we need to rebalance the portfolio to address new goals? When a client focuses on the bigger picture and the end result—

financial independence—they want to achieve. Nobody has a crystal ball that looks into the future. But hindsight is always twenty-twenty.

While the stock market doesn't rise every year, it has risen 70 percent of the time between 1926 and 2022.[59] That's why it is important to look at historical financial data and charts. Historically, the stock market has averaged a 10 percent gain before inflation is factored in. However, between 1926 and 2022, returns were in the "average" band of 8–12 percent only seven times.[60] The rest of the time they were much lower or usually much higher. So, volatility is a natural state in the stock market, which is why understanding the history of a particular stock, bond, mutual investment, or other financial instrument is imperative to maintaining calm emotions.

Here is a historical chart for the TSX:

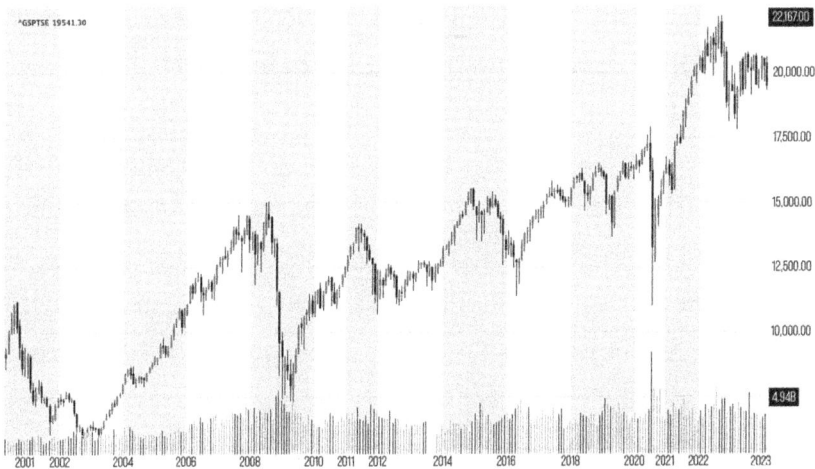

Wikipedia, The Free Encyclopedia, "S&P/TSX Composite Index," accessed April 15, 2024, https://en.wikipedia.org/wiki/S%26P/TSX_Composite_Index.

---

59   James Royal, "What Is the Average Stock Market Return?" March 5, 2024, https://www.nerdwallet.com/article/investing/average-stock-market-return.

60   Ibid.

As you can see, despite the ups and downs, since 1995, the overall trend has been up. Charts such as these are available for almost all financial investment instruments. I use this type of historical data to show my clients that if they sell during a downturn and don't reinvest soon enough, it will take a long time to recoup their losses. This is why I say that part of my job is to be a "voice of reason" for my clients.

Different Clients, Different Perspectives

One of the things I enjoy most about being a wealth management advisor is that I have different clients who have different needs. This means that I have to be open-minded and to really listen and hear my clients' goals and objectives. For instance, if I have a young client with a young family, their needs will be much different than a client who is approaching retirement. However, the key to financial independence for all of my clients is diversification.

The great thing about diversification is that it applies to all market sectors and to all financial investments. For instance, for a young family, it might be that investing in stocks and different types of funds is the best option. Within a stock portfolio, we could invest in Canadian, American, European, or any other publicly traded company. The same applies to funds. For someone approaching retirement, they might be focused on preserving capital, so the bond market, money market accounts, or conservative stocks and funds might be the best option. Once again, my role as an amateur psychologist comes into play. It is my job to understand my client's makeup. Are they risk-averse? Are they willing to ride the volatility that comes with high risk/high reward investments? Are they somewhere in between? My client's outlook in finances will go a long way in determining what their investment portfolio looks like and how diversified it is within the sectors they are investing in.

Let's say I am working with a young couple with a child and both work entry-level jobs. On the bright side, the couple has their entire future ahead of them. However, their current financial situation demands their full income, and there is very little left over at the end of the month. One of the things I remind the couple is that their income will rise over time, and so will their expenses. But in order to reach financial freedom, they have to take a disciplined approach today that will benefit them in the future. This is where "dollar cost averaging" comes in. Dollar cost averaging is the discipline of investing a fixed amount of money on a regular basis, regardless of the current share price of the investment vehicle. In my view, dollar cost averaging is the most beneficial approach to investing.

For example, a young couple discovers through budgeting that they have an extra $100–$500 every month. Perhaps they want to save for a house. Maybe they want to build their child's education funds. Or they might already be thinking about retirement. (It's never too early to do this.) I would work with the couple to determine the right financial investments that will help them reach their financial goals. As well, I would stress to the couple the importance of compound interest and the way it works over time, no matter what they are investing in.

Here is a chart that shows the importance of dollar cost averaging for this young couple:

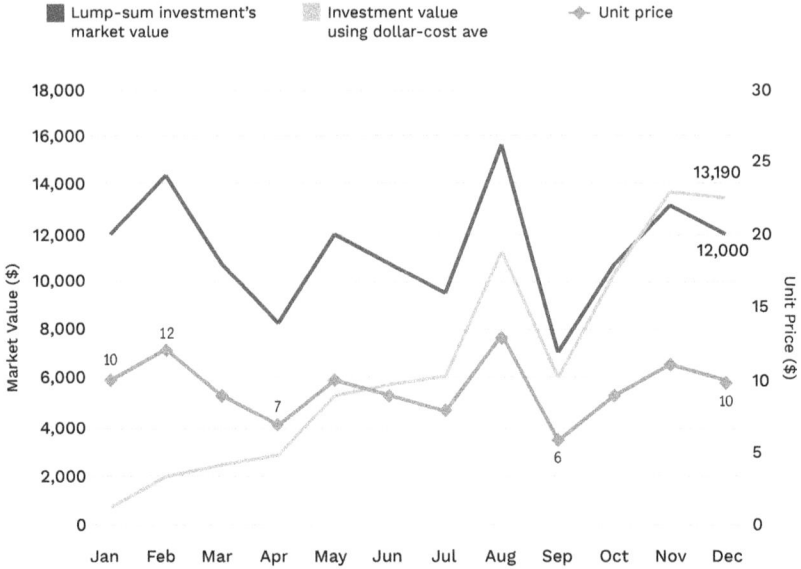

Over time, your average price per unit will be lower than
if you invested all your money at one time.

Note: For illustration purposes only.

Now, let's say I'm working with an older couple. They own their home, their children are out of the house, and they have a solid financial plan in place. However, with the markets in a downturn, and retirement becoming a reality in a few years, they are watching their portfolio lose money before their very eyes. For this couple, I would be reassuring and tell them to stop watching their portfolio so closely. This couple has been dollar cost averaging with their investments for years. We know what type of return on investment they need, and their portfolio is set up to deliver. Whether the market drops 20 percent or goes up 30 percent, dollar cost averaging will bring them the financial freedom they have been planning for. I also remind them that they survived during the major market meltdowns of 2001, 2008, and so on, and their portfolios thrived after these events. Whatever today's markets look like, this couple has been building their financial "Ark" for years, and they need to stay the course.

Here is another chart illustrating the prudence of dollar cost averaging:

Potential Difference of Investing $30,000 as a Lump Sum Versus 12 monthly payments of $2,500

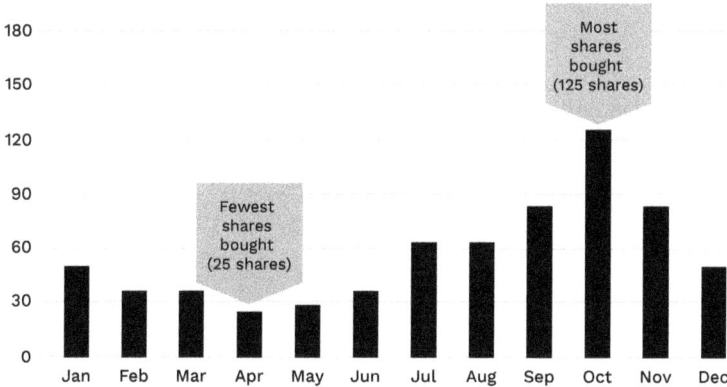

Based upon hypothetical market movements. There is no guarantee that dollar cost averaging will result in better returns than lump sum investing.

	Dollar cost averaging	Lump sum investment
Avg price per share	$44.30	$50.00
Shares accumulated	676.59	600
Value by end of year	$33,830	$30,000

Fidelity Investment Canada, "Potential Difference of Investing $30,000 as a Lump Sum versus 12 Monthly Payments of $2,500."

Finally, I want to talk about the client who has already reached financial freedom. This individual may have a net worth of $10 million, $50 million, or more. On the surface, one wouldn't think this individual would be concerned about market volatility. If the market dropped 10 percent, and the client lost $1 million or $5 million, based on their portfolio, would that really affect their everyday life? This comes down to the individual's personality and mindset. Some clients would fret, and others would say, "That's the way the market goes." This comes down to the individual's personality and mindset.

My point to all of this is that different clients have unique perspectives, and each client must be treated as an individual and not with a "herd" mentality that some investment advisors have. And no matter what a client's net worth may be, or how large their portfolio is, dollar cost averaging works for everyone.

Investing in My Team

Reassuring clients is something I remind my team to do every day. I also reiterate that it is easy to do this when the economy is good but much more important when there is volatility. To help my team, we meet weekly, and oftentimes, I will meet with particular advisors daily. Together, we review their clients' portfolios to make sure their investments are on track with the clients' objectives. I also let my team members know what I am doing with my clients. While my advisors are free to follow my direction or make their own paths, sharing my insights and advice builds trust within my team, and they, in turn, feel comfortable sharing new information with me and with each other.

For instance, I might attend an investment seminar hosted by a fund manager. I will always recap the information with my team. A team member might find a new company that might interest another advisor. I also bring fund managers, life insurance specialists, tax lawyers, and other experts from whom my team and I can learn. My philosophy behind doing all of this is simple: the more input you have, the more opinions you listen to, the more experts you learn from, the greater your own level of experience and expertise.

In my team meetings, the advisors under me are free to ask their questions and express their concerns. For example, a new advisor might be frustrated over their lack of gaining clients; perhaps they lack communication skills and confidence. Even if they have a wealth of financial knowledge, the most important part is to communicate that information to their clients in such a way that the *client* fully understands. A big part of my training is focused on how to clearly deliver the message.

As a team, we are ready to support each advisor and remind them to follow the "recipe" that has been established; it's about the numbers, not the emotion. Most of our advisors start when they are young and enthusiastic. They have a solid educational background and are ready to start their own financial advisory business within Diligence. However, they lack the real-world experience; they haven't been through the volatility of bull and bear markets, nor do they know how to navigate economic events like COVID-19 or a recession that downturn snowball effect throughout the markets. To help all advisors, novice and experienced, our office has a research department that stays on top of current trends and analysis as well as monitoring individual stocks and various types of funds. Each advisor has access to all of this information, so they can do what is best according to the client's financial goals.

For instance, an advisor might have a question about rebalancing a client's portfolio. We hear many different opinions coming from various experts, and it takes a lot of thought and strategizing to make the right decision for our clients. Should we be invested more in the United States, Canada, or international? Should we be more in equities or in bonds? Should we favor value or growth stocks? These are the types of questions we discuss as a team, and then the advisor can give their client the best advice.

As you can see, it can be very confusing, especially for a younger advisor who is fairly new to the business. This is where our training and weekly meetings are very important to make sure that everyone follows the guidance and direction from our research team. I also remind each advisor that they are the calming voice for their clients when the financial markets are volatile and to keep their clients focused on their long-term objectives. I also constantly remind my team that their clients can benefit from opportunities that present themselves in any type of a market. It is a matter of seeing if the opportunity is aligned with the client's portfolio.

What Goes Around Comes Around

One thing that wealth management advisors rarely do is discuss the way they earn their income. In my view, the most honest and forthright way is for advisors to earn their income based on fixed percentages. When the markets are doing well, my team and I can collect good paychecks for doing our jobs well. However, when the markets are doing poorly, our income also drops.

We are paid a percentage of the AUM. While the percentage always remains the same, the AUM varies every day with the market. For instance, if the market gains 1 percent, our income goes up by 1 percent. If the market goes down 1 percent, our income goes down by the same amount. Just like new clients who are watching their portfolio balance drop, new advisors go through the same type of emotional roller coaster regarding their income structure. So, I'm there to remind them that market and income volatility is a fact of life in this business.

No matter what the markets are doing, or how well we are doing as advisors, I constantly remind my team that there are others who are way less fortunate than us. This is the reason why my team and I always help out at a food bank every year, giving of our time and money. It is also the reason why I want to be as benevolent as possible, whenever possible, and I encourage my team to do the same.

The final chapter in this book focuses on your ongoing self-education. Investing for success means different things to different people, and you will be able to clearly see and decide what financial success means to you.

TAKEAWAYS

- It is impossible to predict the future. If we could do that, we would be like Noah when he built the Ark on dry land.
- Chicken Little is decrying, "The sky is falling!" Everyone forgets that economies and financial markets will *rebound*.
- While the stock market doesn't rise every year, it has risen 70 percent of the time between 1926 and 2022.
- The great thing about diversification is that it applies to all market sectors and to all financial investments.
- Dollar cost averaging is the most beneficial approach to investing.

Personal Takeaways

WHAT DID I LEARN? WHAT ARE MY FUTURE STEPS?

_____

_____

_____

_____

_____

_____

_____

_____

_____

_____

_____

_____

_____

_____

_____

_____

_____

_____

_____

_____

_____

_____

_____

_____

CHAPTER 14

INVESTING FOR SUCCESS

Planning is bringing the future into the present
so that you can do something about it.
—ALAN LAKEIN

I nvesting for success is both a science and an art.

It is science, because success comes with having a financial plan, goals to achieve specific outcomes, following what the data show, and keeping emotion out of the picture.

Success is also an art because it's subjective; what one person's definition of success is differs from other people. As an art, success is emotional. There is a great sense of satisfaction that comes with achieving financial goals and outcomes; there's an immense feeling of relief that comes with knowing everything is in order and following a defined path.

Follow the Plan

A financial plan is a document you create with your advisor/planner that starts with a solid understanding of your current financial situation, including your current net worth and cash flow. Next, the plan maps out your short- and long-term goals, along with the strategies—what to invest in and how to invest—to achieve those goals. The plan reflects your unique circumstances and future outlook, taking into consideration your personal and family situations, risk tolerance, and future expectations.

Is having a written financial plan truly important to your financial future? Consider the following chart:

ACCORDING TO A STUDY BY THE FINANCIAL PLANNING STANDARDS COUNCIL, LET'S SEE HOW CANADIANS WITH A COMPREHENSIVE FINANCIAL PLAN COMPARE TO THOSE WITH NO PLAN.

	Comprehensive financial plan	No financial plan
Feel on track with their financial goals	**81%**	**44%**
Feel their ability to save has improved in the past five years	**62%**	**40%**
More confident they can deal with unexpected financial emergencies	**60%**	**28%**

Financial Planning Standards Council, "The Value of Financial Planning, 2012," accessed December 2, 2022, https://www.scotiabank.com/ca/en/personal/advice-plus/features/posts.5-reasons-financial-plan.html.

Here is even more reason to "stick with the plan":

> The financial crisis of late 2008 and early 2009 when stocks dropped nearly 50 percent might have seemed a good time to run for safety in cash. But a Fidelity study of 1.5 million workplace savers found that those who stayed invested in the

stock market during that time were far better off than those who headed for the sidelines.[61]

In the decade following the start of the crisis in June 2008, those who stayed invested saw their account balances—which reflected the impact of their investment choices and contributions—grow 147 percent. That's twice the average 74 percent return for those who fled stocks during the fourth quarter of 2008 or first quarter of 2009. While most investors did not make any changes during the market downturn, those who did made a fateful decision with a lasting impact. More than 25 percent of those who sold out of stocks never got back into the market and missed the gains that followed.[62]

Finally, when asked how prepared you are (were) for retirement, a Canadian survey showed the following, regarding the importance of having a written financial plan:

The Importance of a Written Financial Plan
86% OF CANADIANS WITH A WRITTEN FINANCIAL PLAN WORKED WITH A FINANCIAL ADVISOR TO BUILD IT.

	Financially	Emotionally	Physcially	Socially
WITH A PLAN	90%	89%	90%	87%
DIFFERENCE	31%	17%	15%	15%
WITHOUT A PLAN	59%	72%	72%	75%

Fidelity Investments Canada, "The Importance of a Written Financial Plan," 2021.

---

61   Fidelity blog, "6 Habits of Successful Investors," accessed December 1, 2023, https://www.fidelity.com/viewpoints/investing-ideas/six-habits-successful-investors.

62   Ibid.

Habits of a Successful Investor

As with anything that is worth doing, financial habits need to be established—and stayed with!—in order to achieve success. Here are some habits that can lead to the financial success you envision.

- Set clear, measurable, and attainable investment goals. Short-term goals should be revised and replaced as they are achieved, and all short-term goals should lead to long-term success. Long-term goals should be left in place, for exactly that—the long term. The following chart shows what happens when a short-term focus replaces a long-term mindset.

Frequent Portfolio Evaluation Can Lead to Risk Averse Behaviour

A SHORT-TERM FOCUS CAN LEAD TO INVESTING TOO CONSERVATIVELY.

Constant reminders of volatility may cause investors to seek more conservative investments, regardless of objectives or time horizon.

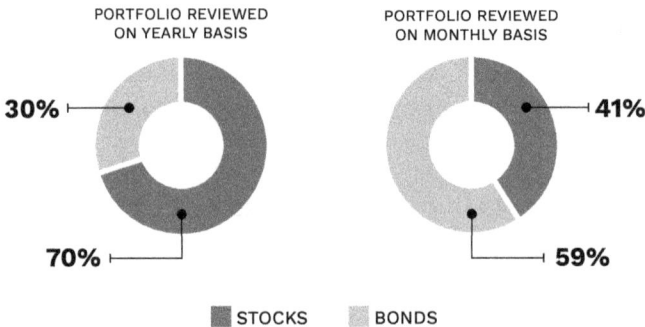

PORTFOLIO REVIEWED ON YEARLY BASIS

30%

70%

PORTFOLIO REVIEWED ON MONTHLY BASIS

41%

59%

STOCKS   BONDS

In the study, subjects were assigned simulated conditions that were similar to making portfolio decisions on a monthly or yearly basis.

Richard H. Thaler, et al., "The Effect of Myopia and Loss Aversion on Risk Taking: An Experimental Test," The Quarterly Journal of Economics 112, no. 2 (1997), used by permission of Manulife via Fidelity Investments who received permission from Oxford University Press.

- Have a balanced investment portfolio. When the markets are doing well, investors jump in. When the markets are in a downturn, investors jump out. However, having the right mix of assets—stocks, bonds, ETFs, cash, etc.—will reflect reasonable expectations based on your risk tolerance. The key word is "balanced." All investments involve risk of loss, so it's important to understand the investments that make up your portfolio and why these are chosen.

- Both asset allocation and diversification are rooted in the idea of balance. Because all investments involve risk, investors must manage the balance between risk and potential reward through the choice of portfolio holdings.

- Have a good understanding of saving and spending. You can spend yourself into debt that can take years to pay off, which can severely hamper your retirement plans. Conversely, you can be so "retirement rich" that you become "current life poor." What I mean is that it's important to spend within reason in the present so that you enjoy life on the way to accomplishing your retirement

> **Both asset allocation and diversification are rooted in the idea of balance.**

goals. To help accomplish a balance between your current lifestyle and future retirement, your advisor/planner can help you determine what percentage of your income that you can invest for your retirement, along with any employer match, that will allow you to have enough money to pay bills and enjoy life today. As well, it stands to reason that the earlier you follow an investment plan, the earlier you will reach your long-term goals.

- Taxes

  No matter what you do to earn income, the taxman will always come knocking at your door. However, whether you are a business owner or an employee, a competent financial advisor/ planner will help you find and use all legal deductions to reduce your tax exposure and generate higher after-tax returns. Where you put your money into what types of accounts and investments based on tax savings is called "asset location." This includes utilizing maximum use of RRSPs, TFSAs, and RESPs (registered education savings plans); income and/or pension splitting with your spouse or common law partner; principle and secondary residence exemption; first-time home ownership amount[63] moving expenses; the Canada caregiver credit;[64] medical expenses;[65] and charitable donations.[66]

- Overcoming greed

  There is a crude but true saying in the stock market world, "Bulls make money and bears make money, but pigs never do." There is another saying as well: "Leave money on the table." What these sayings mean is that once you have reached your short- and long-term goals, don't keep saying to yourself, "If I stay in just a while longer, I can make much more money." Always remember

---

63 Canadians can claim $5,000 if you or your spouse or common-law partner acquired an existing home or one under construction. However, you must not have lived in another home owned by you, your spouse, or common-law partner in the year of, or prior four years, acquiring the new home.

64 Government of Canada, "The Canada Caregiver Credit," last modified January 18, 2021, https://www.canada.ca/en/revenue-agency/services/tax/individuals/topics/about-your-tax-return/tax-return/completing-a-tax-return/deductions-credits-expenses/canada-caregiver-amount.html.

65 Only expenses that you have not or will not be reimbursed for can be claimed.

66 Tax credits of up to 33 percent of a donation at the federal level and further provincial credits available; claims of up to 75 percent of net income and donations can be carried forward for up to five years.

that if you stay invested longer than planned for, you can lose money and lose it fast, if the market takes a sudden downturn.

- Understanding market uncertainties

  Anyone who tells you that they can predict the future of an asset or what the market will do is akin to a shyster; they are simply after your money. All investments come with a risk of uncertainty. No one can foretell with accuracy what will happen in future markets. However, honest and competent financial advisors/planners do their research and bring as much knowledge as possible to help guide your investment plan.

- Make more by accepting losses

  When markets drop, there are times to stay in and use a dollar cost averaging strategy. In the long run, this will reduce your cost per share or asset and will set you up for long-term gains. There are also times to accept a loss on one investment in order to benefit from a gain in another asset. An astute advisor/ planner will help you determine when to use these strategies.

- Discipline, discipline, discipline

  If you were on a diet to lose weight, you would have to be disciplined. If you were going to the gym to get in shape, you'd have to be disciplined. If you were going to complete any plan, you would have to remain disciplined to achieve your goals. Financial planning is no different. And the number one key to financial discipline is to set up regular deposits in your investment account as part of your financial alloca- tion. Here's proof. The following chart shows that a $10,000 investment can become $5,020 by missing out on sixty of a market's best days, based on annualized returns in the S&P/ TSX Composite Index:

$10,000 Invested from January 1986 to December 2020

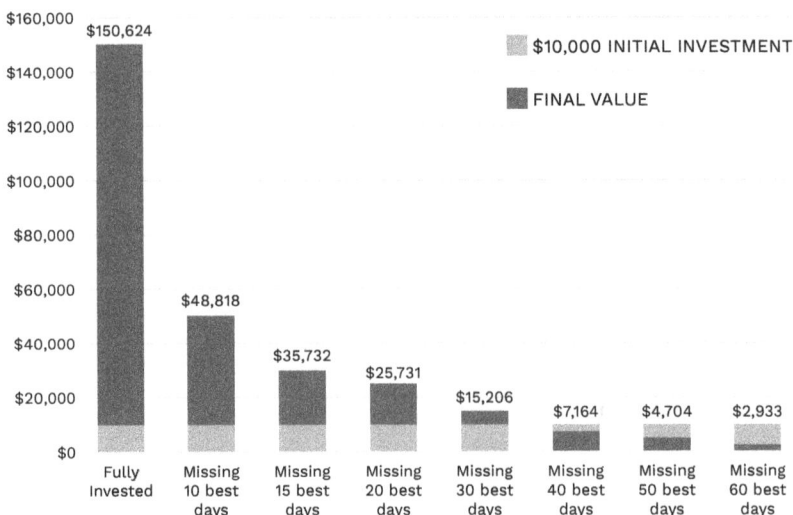

| | $10,000 INITIAL INVESTMENT |
| | FINAL VALUE |

Bar chart showing values:
- Fully Invested: $150,624
- Missing 10 best days: $48,818
- Missing 15 best days: $35,732
- Missing 20 best days: $25,731
- Missing 30 best days: $15,206
- Missing 40 best days: $7,164
- Missing 50 best days: $4,704
- Missing 60 best days: $2,933

Refinitiv, "S&P/TSX Composite Index Total Returns from January 1, 1986, to December 31, 2020," accessed January 10, 2023, https://www.nbfwm.ca/content/ dam/fbngp/microsites/cappelli-wealth-management-group/articles/Three%20 charts%20on%20the%20benefits%20of%20staying%20invested.pdf.

The Power of Compounding

When you start investing is just as important as how you invest.

When you start investing is just as important as *how* you invest. And no matter your age, investing for the future is easy to put off until tomorrow, then the next month, then the next year, and so on. It's human nature not to want to look twenty to thirty years down the road. It's also common to think that if you don't have money to invest today, you can do so at a later date and contribute more to catch up. However, as the following chart illustrates, it is always better to build wealth by starting early, even if you only have limited funds available.

The Power of Compounding

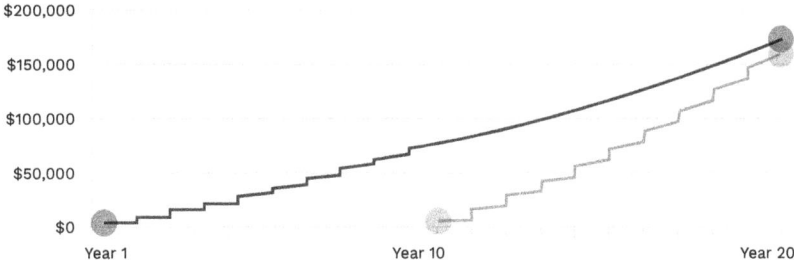

Laura makes ten annual contributions of $5,000 and receives an 8% annual return. She stops investing after ten years, and holds on to the investment for a further ten years, at an 8% annual return.

Joel makes ten annual contributions of $10,000 at an 8% annual return. He ends up with less than Laura, even though he invested twice as much money, because he started later.

So the sooner you invest, the more time your money has to grow and benefit from the power of compounding.

	Laura	Joel
Years contributed	10	10
Years Invested	20	10
Total amount contributed	$50,000	$100,000
Total amount at the end of the period	$168,887	$156,455

This example assumes an 8% annual return during years invested. The rate of return shown is used to illustrate the effects of the compound growth rate and is not intended to reflect future values of the fund or returns on investment in any fund.

Investment Options to Consider

As a wealth management advisor, new and established clients often ask, "What do you recommend?" It is my job to help guide my clients to determine what investments are the most prudent for their portfolios to achieve their short- and long-term goals. Depending on their needs here is my advice.

STOCKS

Very common to every portfolio, stocks are also called "equities" because it is a security that represents ownership. People tend to buy well-known companies because it gives them a sense of comfort, knowing that these companies have a long history of growth. Stocks are for long-term investors because they are unpredictable and can be very volatile. They are also a hedge for inflation. When you buy a share of a company, you become an "owner," giving you voting privileges, access to company information, and you can even become a board member.

Recommendation

I wouldn't recommend buying stocks on your own, because volatility in the markets can make you emotional, which can lead to making mistakes, that is, selling or buying at the wrong time. Purchasing individual stocks should be managed by a professional money manager, who has your best interests in mind.

BONDS

Bonds are similar to a stock but much more secure and less volatile because these are considered "debt" the company owes you, called "corporate debt," not equity. In other words, if you hold a company's bond, that company owes you your money and will repay you the full principal amount at the maturity date. Until the maturity date, you are paid a contracted interest rate. Bonds are very sensitive to interest rates; when interest rates drop, bond prices rise.

For example, in 2022, typical bond value fell 13 percent[67] because the central bank rate rose about sixteen-fold.[68] When interest rates go up, bonds drop in value because we assume that the next bond issuance will pay a better interest rate. As well, a bond can have a fixed or variable rate, depending on the type of bond being issued.

Recommendation

Bonds are a solid investment as the following chart shows:

It's Rare to Have Two Consecutive Years of Negative Returns for Bonds

US TREASURY AND US CREDIT INDEX 1974 – 2022

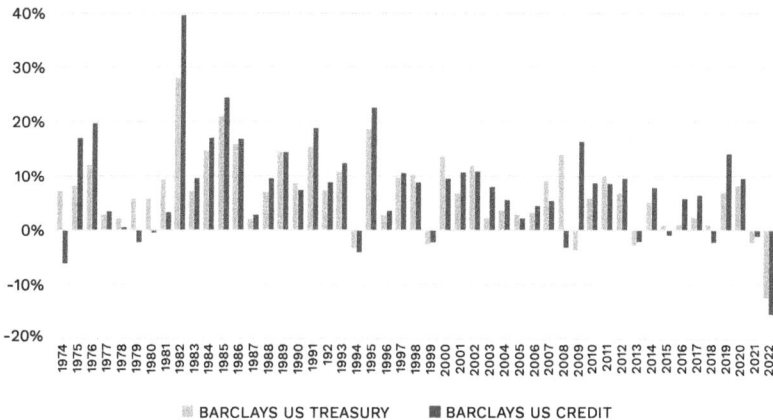

BARCLAYS US TREASURY　　BARCLAYS US CREDIT

Bloomberg, "It's Rare to Have 2 Consecutive Years of Negative Returns for Bonds," chart, Manulife Investment Management, Capital Markets Strategy, December 31, 2022, In Manulife Chartbook, Q1, 2023, accessed January 20, 2023, https://global-pacific.com/system/files/Chartbook%20Q2%202022_3.pdf.

67　Great Lacurci, "2022 Was the Worst-Ever Year for U.S. Bonds. How to Position for 2023," CNBC, January 7, 2023, https://www.cnbc.com/2023/01/07/2022-was-the-worst-ever-year-for-us-bonds-how-to-position-for-2023.html.

68　"Open Market Operations," Federal Reserve, accessed April 12, 2023, https://www.federalreserve.gov/monetarypolicy/openmarket.htm.

You can buy your own bonds if you do your own due diligence, but this can become very complex when looking at the duration, credit rating, and political/economic climate. Although the only risk to a bond is the company's credit risk if you keep it until maturity, I recommend going through your advisor, who should know the best types of bonds for your portfolio.

DIVIDEND GROWTH STOCKS

Investing in dividend growth stocks is a great way to diversify your portfolio so that you can hedge against market downturns and inflation. Company stocks that offer dividends are stable with low volatility and offer long-term growth potential. A dividend is the portion of a company's earnings that is paid out to shareholders. When a company makes a profit, it shares its earnings with investors on a scheduled basis, such as quarterly or annually. The dividend can either be taken as a cash payout or can be reinvested into the company through stock purchases.

Recommendation

These stocks are an excellent and conservative invest-ment vehicle.

MUTUAL FUNDS

Mutual funds were very popular from the 1980s to the early 2000s, but they are a lot less attractive now as ETFs exist. The fund companies and advisors now have the obligation to clearly disclose the MER (Management Expense Ratio) of each fund to the client. In prior years, the big problem with mutual funds was the hidden fees (front end, back end, MER, etc.). Also, within the North American investment advisors/planners community, history shows that over 90 percent of mutual funds never beat the market on a consistent basis. It is very difficult to pick the right fund because a fund manager can be a hero one year and a goat the following year. It is very difficult to constantly beat the market. One of the few managers who has done that consistently was the legendary Peter Lynch from Fidelity in the 1980s. While he averaged 29.2 percent in his Magellan fund between 1977 and 1990, individual investors lost money on the fund because they tried to time the markets (going in and out of the fund to try to avoid losses). Choosing the right mutual fund without professional help is difficult, and staying invested for the long haul is even more difficult!

Recommendation

Stay away from mutual funds if you don't personally know the fund manager. Even though mutual funds have lowered their MERs in recent years, they are still more expensive than ETFs and there is not much added value offered. If you do invest in mutual funds, make sure to hire an investment advisor who knows what they are doing, or else you might wake up in ten years asking yourself where all of your ROI (return on investment) went!

ETF

ETFs became very popular in the last fifteen years because anyone can buy them on any exchange through an online broker. The MERs (the fees charged) are very low because most of these funds are passively managed, meaning that there is not a big group of managers to pay for their investment decisions. There are now thousands of different ETFs to choose from, which can make the decision-making process overwhelming to the uninformed investor. It is also impossible to know which funds will perform the best in the next year or over the next decade, so diversification remains the golden rule, unless you buy one ETF that integrates everything you need in one solution. In that case, you could invest all your money in one fund and potentially earn a good ROI over the long term while only paying an MER of around 0.2 percent

Recommendation

As with mutual funds, an individual investor who tries to manage their portfolio by themselves to avoid paying an advisor is at risk of making emotional decisions. When the markets are doing well, everyone seems to become a financial expert, but when the markets go down, most of the same "experts" disappear. Personally, I am a big fan of ETFs for my clients because the MERs are reasonable and there is a big selection across a wide range of investments. An experienced advisor can make sure that you buy the right ETFs to maximize your gains.

STRUCTURED NOTES

Structured notes are a very complex investment instrument for most people. A structured note is a debt security that has two parts: a bond component and a derivative component. Structured notes can give you exposure to a specific sector or market while limiting your risk.

The note can give you a guaranteed rate of return if certain conditions are met.

Here is an example. A five-year structured note will pay a cumulative 16.85 percent interest yearly, if and when the Canadian bank index is at 0 percent or more on the anniversary date. When this happens, you get back your capital plus interest. If this happens at the second anniversary date, you will get 33.70 percent; at the third anniversary date, you get 50.55 percent; and so on.

Recommendation

As you can see, structured notes can be very attractive, but I would highly discourage anyone from buying these investments without professional help. They are complex investments, and choosing the right bond/derivative component for your portfolio takes both knowledge and experience.

GUARANTEED INVESTMENT CERTIFICATE

When purchasing a Guaranteed Investment Certificate (GIC), an individual deposits a sum of money with a financial institution for a specified period of time. The institution guarantees a specific rate of return plus principal upon maturity of the GIC. I often refer to GICs as a Guaranteed Poverty Certificates because a GIC rate of return will rarely beat the rate of inflation. GICs are often offered by an advisor at your local bank. Most often, the advisor has limited investment experience and was told to sell a set number of GICs each month because they are very profitable for the bank. In my opinion, these products shouldn't even exist! The money invested in a GIC is then used by the bank to invest in better paying investments, with the bank keeping the profit. The GIC also distributes interest income, which is highly taxable in a nonregistered account.

Recommendation

Consult an investment advisor who is completely objective when giving advice before purchasing a GIC. There are always better investments with higher ROIs. For example, the following chart shows that bonds are a much better investment than GICs:

Bonds Outperform GICs Nearly 80% of the Time

DIFFERENCE BETWEEN BANK OF CANADA 1-YEAR GIC RATES VS.
1 YEAR ROLLING CANADIAN FTSE UNIVERSE BOND INDEX

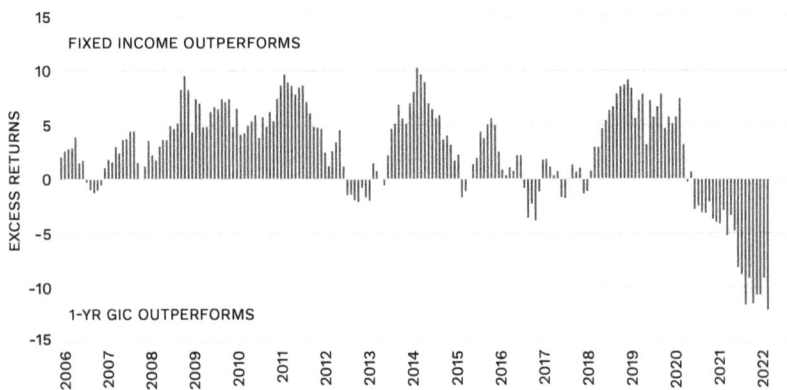

The FTSE 1 Year Rollings returns have been lagged to illustrate the GIC rate at that time. Indices are unmanaged and cannot be purchased directly by investors.

Past performance is not indicative of future results.

Bloomberg, "Bonds Outperform GICs Nearly 80% of the Time," chart, Manulife Investment Management, Capital Markets Strategy, December 31, 2022, in Manulife Chartbook, Q1, 2023, accessed January 23, 2023, https://www.manulifeim.com/retail/ca/en/viewpoints/capital-markets-strategy/bonds-vs-gics.

PRIVATE EQUITY OR DEBT

Usually for sophisticated investors only, this type of investment requires you to make a certain income or to have a certain net worth to qualify.

Private equity or debt is considered risky because the investment vehicle has not yet gone through all the compliance and regulation of a publicly traded company. The ROI is usually adjusted to risk, making private equity or debt potentially more profitable than publicly traded stocks. I have known people to make ten-to-twenty times their investment. This can happen when the company goes public because of the number of shares the investor already owns.

Private debt is very similar, but instead of making a return on the future valuation, a set interest income is earned, usually around 12 percent.

It can be risky to invest in private companies because they are usually smaller companies and in the start-up phase. Also, you need to be fortunate enough to hear about the opportunity, because good deals do not spread like wildfires; they are usually offered to friends and family first.

Recommendation

Find one or two brokers who specialize in private deals so that they can inform you when an interesting company comes along. However, do not limit yourself to one deal, because you never know which company is the next Apple or Walmart. I would recommend diversifying your private equity/dept portfolio into multiple deals to lower your risk and to make sure you get a good overall return.

REAL ASSETS

Timberland, farmlands, and infrastructures like bridges, power plants, etc., are examples of real assets. It can be difficult to invest in real assets without going through a fund or a broker, but these products are very good for diversification. You can invest in a real asset fund with as little as $25,000. An experienced advisor will have a couple of ideas for you.

Warning

Real assets are a good diversification, but like other assets, they shouldn't be your only investment. You can purchase your own real asset by buying land and enjoying it at the same time, something I have done. However, if this is not your goal, it is best to purchase a real asset fund through a professional investment manager.

TAKEAWAYS

- Your financial plan reflects your unique circumstances and future outlook, taking into consideration your personal and family situations, risk tolerance, and future expectations.

- Investing for success is established on financial habits that include setting clear, measurable, and attainable investment goals; having a balanced investment portfolio; a good understanding of saving and spending; understanding tax liabilities and deductions; overcoming greed; understanding there will be market uncertainties; making more using dollar cost averaging or by accepting limited losses in order to invest in other opportunities; and, above all, staying disciplined to your plan and following that plan.

■ The answer to the question, "What do you recommend?" is dependent upon what is needed to achieve your short- and long-term goals.

Personal Takeaways

WHAT DID I LEARN? WHAT ARE MY FUTURE STEPS?

_____

_____

_____

_____

_____

_____

_____

_____

_____

_____

_____

_____

_____

_____

_____

_____

_____

_____

_____

_____

_____

_____

_____

_____

_____

_____

_____

CONCLUSION

As you come to the closing of this book, I trust you've enjoyed reading it as much as I've enjoyed writing all of this material just for you!

Whether you choose to hire a wealth management advisor, or decide to make your own investment decisions, it is crucial that you maintain two mindsets at all times: making profits, even if this means taking a more conservative approach to investing and mitigating losses through tax strategies, and proactive—versus reactive—decision-making regarding when to move your investment money. Keep in mind that emotions should not rule your decisions. Nor can you try to time the market. Doing so will cause you to lose more money than you will ever make.

There will always be unprecedented events that affect the markets—both good and bad—and these are unforeseeable. Therefore, having a plan and sticking to that plan is the best path to follow. The saying, "Fools rush in where angels fear to tread," aptly applies to financial investment decision-making. While no one ever wants to "lose" money in the markets, every wise investor and every prudent investment plan takes into account that there will always be market "ups and downs" and emotions such as fear or greed cannot be accommodated, if financial success is to be achieved.

Thierry and Francis visiting a local vineyard while attending a conference in California and celebrating with other successful advisors from across Canada, 2023.

Here are two things to always keep in mind:

- Have some rules to follow and tools to use that are beneficial when setting up and staying with an investment plan.

- There are more ways to lose money in the market than there are ways to make money, and allowing emotions to rule decision-making is the chief way to lose money.

In closing, if you have benefited from this book, I'd love to hear from you. If you know of someone who can benefit from this book, feel free to share your copy, or better yet, purchase one for them—in doing so, you'll be investing in their financial future. As well, if you, or someone you know, would like to have an initial consultation with my team or me, feel free to contact us at: www.FrancisGroy.com.

Here's to your financial success!

Francis Gingras Roy

ABOUT THE AUTHOR

From his early days as a wealth management advisor, Francis Gingras Roy has distinguished himself year after year as a knowledgeable, astute, and prudent Investment Advisor. He has won several honourable mentions from his brokerage firm, including participation in the Circle of Excellence and the President's Circle. Indeed, Francis's vision and work ethic are the catalyst to ranking him among the best in the country. He has made the Wealth Professional Canada's Top 50 Advisors list in 2020, 2021, and 2022, as well as being named a Globe and Mail 5-Star Advisor in 2021. He was also recognized in the *Globe and Mail*'s top Canadian Wealth Management Advisors in 2022.

Francis's mission is to help as many Canadians as possible achieve and exceed their financial goals. He specializes in the management of assets of individuals with significant wealth, management companies, and family trusts. His clients include active professionals and retired couples and individuals. Francis is also co-owner of Diligence Wealth Management and a real estate investor.

Francis lives in Montreal, Quebec, with the love of his life, Audrey Ann, and their beautiful daughters, Sofia and Olivia.

For more information, visit www.francisgroy.com.